GW00836595

The Long March

How the left won the culture war
and what to do about it

The Long March

How the left won the culture war

and what to do about it

Marc Sidwell

The
New
Culture
Forum

Designed by sarahbettsworthdesign@talktalk.net
Printed and bound in the United Kingdom

ISBN   978-1-9993475-1-2

Published by the New Culture Forum

New Culture Forum
55 Tufton Street
London SW1P 3QL
www.newcultureforum.org.uk

For my parents,
and all the millions of teachers and academics
who, like them, pass on a love of learning

CONTENTS

ACKNOWLEDGEMENTS

To write about the long march is to attempt a tightrope walk. To some, the cultural conquest of Britain's institutions is too obvious to need restating. To others, the idea is right-wing paranoia, its bogeyman little more than a wisp summoned by the conspiratorial imagination. I have tried to offer a take worth reading, whatever your perspective. Even if you deny the reality of a cultural takeover, it is the lived experience of many Conservatives, a primary concern of major commentators of the right, and it will shape decisions at the highest levels of political power in the years ahead. It is a concept that must be taken seriously. If you are already convinced that we are the victims of a Gramscian plot, I hope that the complex history I explore will reveal a more surprising pattern of causation – and offer unexpected grounds for hope.

More people than I can name have been incredibly generous with their time and insight as I worked on this book. Above all, my thanks go to Peter Whittle and the New Culture Forum for giving me the opportunity to develop my thoughts – and being patient when life got in the way. Special thanks to John O'Sullivan for agreeing to write a foreword. The edits of Clive Liddiard improved the end result immeasurably, and Matt Luck prepared the handsome index.

By great good fortune, as I was beginning my research in the summer of 2019, the Battle of Ideas charity hosted its Academy on 'Culture Wars: Then and Now'. The weekend at Wyboston Lakes was stimulating, informative and delightfully collegial. My thanks to Angus Kennedy, Geoff Kidder and all those involved. I am especially grateful to Professor James Tooley, whose lecture on the history of state schools drew my attention to the shifting ideological motivations that have shaped education policy in Britain, from the missionary zeal of early inspectors to the 2019 statutory guidelines on sex education.

The experience of those who fought heroic earlier battles on the cultural front lines was also invaluable. My particular thanks go to Lord Pearson of Rannoch, who saw first-hand the dangers of an ideological takeover in teacher training, as well as Baroness Cox of Queensbury. Lady Cox's account of the campaign to radicalise the Polytechnic of North London, composed with Keith Jacka and John Marks, is a vital source for anyone who wishes to see the 'Long March' strategy with the mask off. The historian Robert Service offered perspective on the bigger picture of Soviet subversion, based on his unparalleled knowledge of Cold War archives.

As I turned to the opportunities for the formation of new institutions, the entrepreneurial and creative energy of America's culture warriors was impossible to ignore. I learned a great deal from the novelist and *Daily Wire* podcast host Andrew Klavan, and the Claremont Institute continues to be an extraordinary example of how to combine intellectual heft with effective influence.

My conclusions owe a special debt to the thought of James Davison Hunter on the mechanisms of cultural change, and Timur Kuran on the power of preference falsification to control expression even in a free society. The online essays of Kevin Simler on the *Melting Asphalt* blog also influenced my thinking on mechanisms of persuasion. For anyone interested in further reading, 'Ads Don't Work That Way' and 'Here Be Sermons' are well worth your time.

Finally, this book was composed under a weight of personal circumstance, which the support of family and friends did more to lighten than they can know.

All errors, of course, are my own. 𝆑

FOREWORD: Making democracy irrelevant

John O'Sullivan

Early in this short but formidable book, an important question is asked and answered. It relates to the successive decisions by Conservative education ministers from 2016 onwards to introduce mandatory sex and relationship education in primary and secondary schools. Such compulsion marked a radical change in Tory attitudes to parental rights and is plainly in conflict with the 1948 UN Declaration of Human Rights, which protects such rights. To make such an objection is to stand beneath a warm waterfall of soothing ministerial assurances that any hard edges in the law will be smoothed away when the statutory guidance on its interpretation is eventually published. When the statutory guidance was published last year, however, it included these instructions to schools and teachers:

> Schools should be alive to issues such as everyday sexism, misogyny, homophobia and gender stereotypes and take positive action to build a culture where *these are not tolerated, and any occurrences are identified and tackled*. [my italics]

I might describe that guidance as the Section 28 of the 'Woke' revolution. But that would be to make light of the matter. Section 28 prohibited local authorities from 'promoting' attitudes favourable to homosexuality. This guidance is a great deal more 'authoritarian'. It proposes to repress, or even eradicate, dissenting attitudes on sex and gender from education – irrespective of whether those attitudes are Christian, Muslim or informed by the overwhelming evidence of the physical and social sciences that 'gender stereotypes' reflect real biological differences, and that the traditional family ensures better outcomes for those children raised in it than do alternative family structures.

Many people will side with Tory ministers and their 'Blob' of bureaucratic handlers on specific issues here. And it's true that some religious attitudes have fostered prejudice – though they also inspired Christians to overcome prejudice and become missionaries for causes such as ending slavery or urban poverty. It is true, too, as Mr Sidwell rightly underscores, that the Sixties revolution – which was broadly liberal, far more than it was radical or progressive – brought greater freedom and social acceptance to minorities, both ethnic and sexual. But the specific content of the guidance should matter less than the fact that the state is here proposing a programme of compulsory indoctrination. In the Blob's own lingo, it seeks to 'build a culture' where the beliefs and values of large minorities – perhaps even a majority of the population taken together – are to be treated as unlawful or as unworthy of support and eradicated from their children. That is bound to produce resistance from respectable religious families – as indeed it has done – which may not be easily repressed. In short, it's a violation of almost everything Toryism is supposed to be about: liberty, cultural and religious tradition, tolerance, prudence and good practical government.

So where on earth did Justine Greening, the minister who introduced this reform, get the idea?

The *short* answer is that she got it from György Lukács, the distinguished Marxist philosopher, who began his career as deputy commissioner for culture in Béla Kun's communist regime in 1919 Hungary. In the brief three months that the regime existed, Lukács wasted no time in instituting a sex education programme in schools, with the aim of overturning bourgeois, Christian sexual morality. Lukács lost power when the regime fell, and his cultural reforms were reversed. But his ideas of sex education lived on as one important ingredient in a cocktail of radical ideas that emphasised cultural, rather than economic, revolution and that theorised that it could be pursued within existing institutions.

The *long* answer is the subject of this book. *The Long March* tells the story of what these ideas were, who developed them, how they spread, and how they have become so dominant in life, thought and politics that Tory ministers can utter them with only a slight risk of the blowback that truly Tory ideas would meet. It's a biography of what has become generally known as cultural Marxism (though it has gone under various ideological labels in its time). And it's an absorbing story of the unlikely, interesting and clever people who pioneered these ideas in both unpromising and oddly favourable circumstances.

Lukács was one of them – he had a long career in both radical philosophy and revolutionary politics; but he was not the most important. That was Antonio Gramsci, a communist in one of Mussolini's prison cells, who in the 1930s had the insight that the left could never win power over the opposition of cultural institutions like universities, the media and the Church, as their conservative ideas exercised a 'hegemony' over the minds of people. That hegemony would have to be broken – or better, transformed into a revolutionary one. Meanwhile, in the United States of the 1940s, German academics fleeing from Hitler identified popular culture – Hollywood movies, in particular – as wielding a pervasive influence that conditioned the masses into an acceptance of capitalist society. Max Horkheimer and Theodor Adorno maintained that the cultural influence and similar forms of disguised power in academia, the law and the press would have to be unmasked by what they called 'critical theory' – though it was critical only of the ideas, history, theories and institutions of Western liberal capitalist societies: it was defensive of Soviet and Third World dictatorships, and notably lacked any interest in self-criticism. Quite the contrary. Its evolving theory held that the only way we could get to genuine free speech was by silencing speech the left disliked. Herbert Marcuse, who in the mid-1960s advanced this doctrine of 'repressive tolerance', claimed that free speech could legitimately be denied to liberal and conservative movements, since they represented a deeper intolerance. He briefly became a media celebrity, as he explained all this to respectful journalists and worshipful student 'rebels'.

Such ideas were still exotic novelties, largely confined to academia, although the English journalist Henry Fairlie noted that under the carapace of Eisenhower's stability, Freudianism was spreading throughout the American middle class in the

Fifties, and predicted that this would prove inconsistent with family stability *in the long run*. The Frankfurt School played a large part in this spread, since, as Mr Sidwell explains lucidly, its blend of Marxism and Freudianism in 'Freudomarxism' was a contribution to revolutionary thought as important as Gramsci's hegemony. It undermined the self-confidence of the middle classes in their moral beliefs, and even in their own virtue. And then Fairlie's '*long run*' proved quite short: the Vietnam War, the *manifestations* in Paris, the student revolt (largely unresisted) across Western universities, and a hundred other signs of what Roger Scruton later divined as the 'repudiation' of the West weakened all institutions, public and private, and opened the doors to the generation of rebellious 'Sixty-Eighters' who walked through them into the corridors of institutional power.

Rudi Dutschke, a German revolutionary, laid out the strategy for this next stage of revolution. Since street revolution and violent terrorism had failed and would fail (though it would keep being tried by Red, Angry and Antifa Brigades), a new respectable kind of rebel would enter the bourgeois world, rise in its universities, teach at its colleges, reinterpret its religious gospels, write its plays, films and sitcoms, shape its laws, devise codes of conduct to implement them in business, and gradually establish a Gramscian cultural hegemony over society, even while the economic institutions remained capitalist in form. That was the long march through the institutions. And though Dutschke did not live to see it, it triumphed. Only those institutions that are simply democratic – principally elected assemblies – have remained beyond the control of the former rebels (although the latter are moving relentlessly to subvert, weaken and render them irrelevant to governing). A low-intensity civil war now rumbles on between cultural power and political power throughout the West – which explains, among many other things, why Tory ministers get up in parliament and propose the educational reforms of György Lukács.

Much of this tale has been told before, but Mr Sidwell tells it with verve – accurately and readably – in about half the book. It is the second half that offers his most original insights into the completeness of the Long March's success: in Britain, it incorporated the anti-revolutionary left. The Fabians had been conducting their own long stroll through the institutions since the late nineteenth century, but national culture and institutions as much shaped them as were shaped by them. The Blairite revolution, because it was self-consciously 'modern' and hostile to the left's anti-capitalism, was seen as moderate. But their ahistorical modernism made the Blairites hostile to the actual institutions of the country, which they saw as antiquated impediments to efficiency. Blair and his technical assistant, Gordon Brown, set about changing society by centralising government (even when, as with devolution, they seemed to be decentralising it) – by installing their party loyalists in new and existing institutions, by regulating companies along political and social lines (not excluding health and safety) and by promoting an ideology of managerialism across both public and private sectors to replace the professional ethos that characterised bodies like the legal and medical professions.

The trouble with managerialism, of course, is the managers. If managers rise within an organisation, they arrive in senior positions with an understanding of how that organisation does and should work. That may make them too conservative, in a non-political sense; but it ensures that they will not tear down the place accidentally. If they arrive at the top from outside, they possess a set of useful techniques to improve efficiency, but may lack sympathy toward practices that the profession has developed to preserve its distinctive virtues. This weakness of managerialism was diagnosed in its infancy by the French Marshal Foch, who commented on the graduates of the Saint-Cyr military academy: 'They know everything. Unfortunately, they don't know anything else.' One of the things the managers may not know, moreover, is why a profession exists and what it should be doing. Because they lack this particular knowledge, they fill the gap with the general set of ideas current in the circles in which they move. For managers in the age of Blair, those ideas were a kind of leftish modernism, distilled in codes of conduct, requirements for promotion and mission statements.

Mr Sidwell shows the many dangerous consequences of this. One is the replacement of professional standards by political values, of which there has been a striking example since he wrote. When Emily Maitlis opened a *Newsnight* programme with a blatant piece of editorialising that attacked Boris Johnson, Dominic Cummings and the government over Cummings' alleged breach of the Coronavirus lockdown regulations, there was strong public criticism and many complaints to the BBC. The Corporation responded to its critics by conceding that Maitlis's statement had breached the BBC's duty of impartiality and reminded programme makers of its rules. That amounted to an implicit criticism of Maitlis, who, for whatever reason, did not appear on the following night's programme. Some of her colleagues and other journalists rallied to her defence, however, on the grounds that everything she had said was true. An earlier generation of news editors would have 'binned' Maitlis's statement, on the grounds that she was endorsing one side of a hotly contested debate still in progress. All, some or none of what she had said might, in time, prove to be true – or, less conclusively, might be the final opinion of a substantial majority. But the facts were as yet undetermined. A news report should be rooted in these distinctions. Not only did Maitlis violate them in her editorialising, however, but she went on to speculate that her view of Cummings was shared by 'the country' and (privately) by Boris Johnson himself, and that her view would prevail. Well, perhaps. Who knows? Even if her view does prevail, however, this blend of outright bias and wild speculation bears no relationship to impartial journalism; and if it comes to be seen as embodying BBC news values, then it will erode popular confidence in any judgement that a BBC report reaches on this or any other controversy. That erosion will be further encouraged by reports that Ms Maitlis's colleagues believe the BBC statement to have been 'cowardly' and that she was right. And it's hard not to suspect that what's going on in the absence of professional standards is the emergence of a journalistic groupthink influenced by the general political sympathies of the news-room. The end result of that can be seen in American journalism, where some reporters now argue that an anti-Trump bias should be a professional obligation for those covering politics.

This political distortion now occurs in most English-speaking countries and at all social levels. It can sometimes be sinister – for instance, in the assessments of federal judicial nominees that the American Bar Association (ABA) offers the US Senate for its consideration. Though still disguised as professional judgements, these are now almost all determined by the ABA's progressive ethos. Or it can sometimes be half-comic, as when social workers in Rotherham wanted to prevent an otherwise suitable couple from adopting a child because they were Ukip voters. The longer it goes on without serious resistance, the less we resist or even notice it, and the more its practitioners present political activism as a professional obligation in all professions.

As I was writing this introduction, Richard Horton, editor-in-chief of the medical journal *The Lancet*, appeared on BBC's *Question Time* as a medical expert and passionately denounced the government for taking too complacent a view of the Coronavirus pandemic. Dr Horton had taken the same view as the government only weeks previously, and he should probably have mentioned that. But he is certainly entitled to express his personal opinion. What kind of authority does that opinion have, however? Dr Horton has become well known for advancing the view that doctors as doctors have a professional obligation to become political activists and to engage in civil disobedience whenever they think that a political issue has poor medical consequences for their – or the world's – patients. His editorials in *The Lancet* have made this argument on numerous occasions, but in particular on the topic of climate change, on which he has called for 'activist' journals to follow *The Lancet*'s campaigning example. But there's an obvious difficulty in the idea of transferring medical authority directly into the political sphere. Most major political questions involve a range of considerations: economic, technical, legal, political, etc. Neither doctors nor lawyers can select the aspect that falls under their speciality and tell the rest of us that we're not entitled to a second opinion on it. And as it happens, not all doctors agree with Dr Horton on the medical case against climate change. Yet when two of them submitted a peer-reviewed article disputing an editorial on this theme, he overruled his sub-editors and rejected it. An editor's opinion has to be final for a number of reasons. But rarely is the best way of advancing a scientific argument to silence your critics. And yet when science embraces politics, it will immediately become subject to the temptation to use political methods to win.

Over time, society is 'nudged' by these judgements to live with the politicisation of everything. It's a world that most of us don't want to live in.

Mr Sidwell suggests several ways in which the right (or the non-left) might respond to this undemocratic – and increasingly anti-democratic – leftist structure of ideological power. All are sensible, decent and worthy of support. Together, they would at least help to check this power. I leave it to the reader to judge which they would favour. But the task of restoring a fully democratic society that allows and encourages free opinion and an open debate is a task as formidable as that which faced Gramsci and the Frankfurt School. It may even be more formidable: the Frankfurt School and its British counterparts were able to infiltrate and eventually dominate our social and cultural institutions, because those institutions were at the time run and staffed by people of a genuinely liberal disposition. They did not discriminate against able colleagues on political grounds (even when, like Guy Burgess at the BBC and the Foreign Office, they were actual spies who almost advertised their treason). But those who now run those institutions are more like Mussolini's fascists, who imprisoned Gramsci because they took cultural politics as seriously as he did – the prosecutor said 'for twenty years we must stop this brain from functioning' – and were prepared to be utterly ruthless in waging the culture war. Our new masters show a similar willingness to impose a 'soft authoritarianism' on society, through mechanisms such as 'political correctness' that ban entire topics from academic, political and public debate, and that penalise heretics by depriving them of their jobs, even in activities that have no ideological significance.

In these circumstances, conservatives and liberals must take the route of democratic politics if they are to survive and eventually to triumph. Of course, if we are successful, we will still be confronted with the difficulty that Mr Sidwell outlines at the start: namely, that an elected government will face an intransigent radical establishment that is determined to maintain its independent power and to impose its cultural dogmas on society. In that conflict, however, it labours under some important disadvantages.

The first is that conservatives aim to maintain and improve society, with an attitude of respect towards its prevailing ideas; radicals seek to transform society in line with novel academic theories that, as Mr Sidwell shows, have difficulty in surviving once they are exposed to the light of day. Their dogmas outrage common sense and provoke opposition among those who have either not become true believers or have not been intimidated/bribed into compliance. Just consider the weakness of some of the most significant leftist ideas. It is not true that racism is whatever anyone perceives it to be. It is not reasonable that women must always be believed, whatever the evidence. It is not good public policy that statistics should not be collected if they are likely to contradict leftist preconceptions – for instance, that children prosper equally in all kinds of family structures. It is not possible to believe that all cultures are equal if you believe that all human beings are equal, since some cultures deny human equality and justify treating whole classes of human beings as inherently inferior. And it is self-destructive to think that sovereignty is mythical or trivial or meaningless, when it clearly means having the power to order your own affairs – the very opposite of what the Greeks have been experiencing for the past five years. Most people realise instinctively that these things are nonsense, without requiring much persuasion. Conservatives only lose such battles when we fail to fight them. And Brexit shows that we can win them if we succeed in arousing the voters on an issue *and* in keeping them informed and passionate about the post-electoral battle in order to close the deal.

Another disadvantage for the left is that clever people get bored with dogma. Milton Friedman explained this 40 years ago, when, in an echo of John Stuart Mill, he noted the mass appearance of the stupid conservative. Until the mid to late 1970s he felt he had rarely met any really stupid conservatives

– we're talking about intellectual circles here – but suddenly he was coming across them all the time. He thought this was a specific case of the 'circulation of the elites'. When a dogma is newly established, it enjoys mass allegiance, except among those remnants of the previous (defeated) elite that gradually die out. After a while, however, clever people notice flaws in the dogma and unanticipated consequences of it. Their criticisms grow, and – though most people remain compliant (odd how that word keeps cropping up these days) – their numbers grow, too. Eventually, what were once the 'new' doctrines are challenged and overthrown by even newer ones – at which point, all the conformists, careerists and the simply confused join the new orthodoxy, because that is the safe and profitable thing to do. A new establishment is born with different and more plausible ideas.

Thatcherism enjoyed that 'preference cascade' in the mid-Eighties; Blairism in the 1990s. The difference is that the Thatcherites were content to let their ideas do their own persuading, while the Blairites installed a managerial intelligentsia and *lumpenintelligentsia* to enforce them (just consider the new and politically correct behaviour of the police). All such structures rest ultimately on ideas, however, so that at some point today's opponents of the cultural radical establishment – like Mr Sidwell – will, to their surprise, find that their enemies have fled the field, only returning in hastily stitched-together replicas of the victors' uniforms.

These are early days, but already signs of such a change are appearing. Brexit was, of course, a hidden majority that first enjoyed a preference cascade, then won an electoral victory, and finally hardened into a more self-conscious and formidable political coalition. Are there any signs, however, of the clever, bored intellectuals changing uniform? As yet, not many; but there is one delightfully subtle example from that Vatican of radical secularism, Hollywood, where the original Frankfurt School partisans made their home and against which they directed their first criticisms. In 2016, the Coen brothers produced the comedy *Hail, Caesar!*, a satire on their own industry in the 1950s, in which a group of Marxist scriptwriters kidnap a popular movie star – George Clooney, playing the centurion in a Fifties biblical movie – and subject him to a course of tutorials in the intricacies of Marxism. Another actor, a tap-dancing musical star who is already a covert communist, is saved from the risk of arrest and exposure by a Soviet submarine, which surfaces off Santa Catalina Island and to which the scriptwriters row him in a small boat, through a tempestuous sea. That provides the opportunity for a pictorial satire of socialist realism art, as the actor strikes a heroic Leninist pose in the boat's bows, clutching to his chest his small Pekinese pet dog. Less obvious, but more subversive, is the fact that the professor who instructs Clooney's character in Marxist thought is none other than Herbert Marcuse of 'repressive tolerance' fame (who did in fact live in Southern California in later life, but was not involved in the film industry). Like *Hail, Caesar!* itself, it's a sign that people are laughing at the ideas that still wield hegemony over us. And that's usually the beginning of the end for a ruling doctrine.

That end will be hastened if people read this book. 🖋

CHAPTER ONE

Gramsci's Ghost

At its heart is the story of a life lived through gritted teeth as left-liberalism became the default setting of universities, schools, churches, the BBC, Big Tech, quangos, the third sector, theatre, comedy, medicine and most blue chip companies.
Christopher Snowdon, reviewing Ed West's *Small Men on the Wrong Side of History: The Decline, Fall and Unlikely Return of Conservatism*, 2020

… institutions have gone wrong but, in their current structure, there is no clear way to correct them. Several police forces, for example, have ceased to investigate burglaries … Thus we have a BBC that lectures rather than enlightens; universities that don't prepare students for jobs; hospitals that don't save patients; and a civil service that exists not to implement policies but to frustrate them.
Sunday Telegraph leader column, 23 February 2020

An odd melancholy haunted the Conservative victory in Britain's 2019 general election. Prime Minister Boris Johnson's new majority of 80 MPs was not just decisive, but overwhelming. Even the most cynical Westminster watchers admitted that a fresh decade of Tory power likely lay ahead. But there was a spectre at the feast: a dead Italian Marxist called Antonio Gramsci. As the Tory party and its supporters raised their champagne flutes to the collapse of Jeremy Corbyn's Labour and its hard-left agenda, their hearts were kept down by fear that this victory was superficial. Beneath the surface, a far more important war had already been lost – to *Signore* Gramsci's ruthless disciples.

This fear explains some of the opinion pieces released by prominent figures on the right in the days after the Conservative landslide. For these authors, the sweeping rejection of their political opponents at the ballot box was cold comfort: the left was not in office, but it still held power. In a notable example, historian Andrew Roberts wrote in the *Telegraph* calling for Mr Johnson not just to focus on Brexit or the economy, but to secure future election victories by committing to 'fight the battle for British political culture' – a battle, he argued, that all of Britain's Tory prime ministers since Margaret Thatcher had ducked. It was time, he said, for 'a Gramscian counter-march through the institutions, liberating one after the other from the grip of the Left'.

Mr Roberts was not alone. Mark Wallace, then executive editor (and now chief executive) of the influential *ConservativeHome* website, wrote in the *Sun* that ministers should steel themselves for a bumpy ride, and warned that legacy Labour appointments had left quangos and commissions stuffed with political enemies. The Johnson government appeared to agree. Number 10 quickly announced that it would not be sending ministers to appear on the BBC's *Today* programme, citing its bias against them. Rather than acting as the politically unassailable force it appeared to be on paper, the new government acted as if it was living in occupied territory.

Douglas Carswell, the former Conservative and Ukip MP, wrote an opinion piece on the *1828* website which again cited Mr Gramsci by name and spelled out the same message in stark terms:

> If the Conservatives last week defeated Marx, as personified by Comrade Corbyn and John McDonnell, their next battle must be against Gramsci – as personified by that army of Guardianista quangocrats whose long march through our institutions currently means that we get a left-wing agenda in almost every sphere of public policymaking, irrespective of who we elect.

Even some intellectuals writing for publications of the left agreed. This January, the philosopher John Gray wrote an essay for the *New Statesman* entitled 'Why the Left Keeps Losing'. He, too, spoke of the contrast between Mr Johnson's 'unassailable power in government' and his weakness before the wider culture, claiming that 'British institutions as a whole remain vehicles of progressivist ideology'. Mr Gray again invoked Mr Gramsci, arguing that the mismatch between Mr Johnson's ambition and such institutional progressivism 'places a question mark over whether he will be able to secure the conjunction of political power with cultural legitimacy that Antonio Gramsci, one of the most penetrating 20th-century political thinkers, called hegemony'.

Who – and what – were they talking about? Mr Corbyn's Marxist views were scrutinised and debated from every possible angle through seemingly endless hours of pre-election coverage. But to the general public, neither the idea of a 'long march' through our institutions nor Mr Gramsci means anything. And yet the fear of his influence was still giving some of our top political thinkers sleepless nights – even after shooting dead Mr Corbyn's bright red fox.

This book is an attempt to lift the veil on Mr Gramsci's legacy in British politics, to interrogate why he provokes such fear, and to explore how justified that fear really is.

We will look at his ideas in more detail later, but the essential doctrine driving Gramsci and other 'cultural Marxists' is simple enough. A successful revolution, they claimed, requires not just the seizure of political and economic power, but also conquest of the cultural sphere. Culture – everything from art and entertainment to religion and morality, social and sexual norms – is, they argued, a sort of factory: one that mass-produces consent for our political way of life. Therefore, to undermine free-market capitalism in the West in favour of socialist revolution, cultural Marxists called for likeminded revolutionaries to seize the means of cultural production.

In practice, much of culture is mediated through institutions, from the Church of England and the BBC, to schools and universities. Recognising this, the cultural Marxists also spoke of a 'long march' strategy. Over time, their allies would march through one institution after another, capturing it for their revolutionary views. From then on, these captive institutions would help to spread an insidiously collectivist culture which

3

undermined the capitalist, individualist status quo and built a new consensus for communism or, at least, some sort of democratic socialism.

It was an argument which both sides in the Cold War took seriously. The CIA supported cultural projects in the other direction, notoriously backing the anti-Stalinist left-wing magazine *Encounter* and subsidising an animated version of George Orwell's *Animal Farm*. The abstract expressionist movement also received secret support from the US government for decades. The spooks at Langley were eager to show the world that America's system could produce a kind of art which smashed through the restrictions of the Soviets' socialist realism.

Still, put this way, the ideas of cultural Marxism seem both extreme and abstract, perhaps even distant – one more anachronism left over from the era of mutually assured destruction. In Britain, for anyone under the age of 30, the threat of Soviet communism is no more than a historical curiosity.

Equally, there are those who look at the idea of a culture war and see only an irrelevant sideshow. Boris Johnson did win the 2019 election – arguably without the support of the institutions of cultural power. How much influence, then, do such institutions really exert? Worse yet, is cultural warfare not just an irrelevance, but actually a diversion from the political battlefield? Wouldn't Mr Corbyn's Labour have been a stronger opponent for the Conservatives if it had only set aside identity politics and appealed to its heartland with straightforward policy proposals to make their lives better?

To begin to understand why a historian like Mr Roberts was nonetheless taking the ideas of the cultural Marxists seriously, and worrying about them so much even as Boris Johnson took power, it helps to review a few facts about British politics in 2019, beginning with the *other* Red Wall. The surface chatter of the election was about Labour's Red Wall in the Midlands and the North, which duly crumbled in the face of Mr Johnson's campaign. But political observers with an eye on the longer term worried about a different Red Wall, one stretching not across particular geographical constituencies, but between university campuses and state school classrooms.

The world of British education is dominated by Labour voters. Mr Roberts complained in his *Telegraph* article, 'Why are over 85 per cent of university lecturers left-wing?' And indeed, political monoculture seems to exist across all areas of the education system. Before the 2017 general election, the *Times Educational Supplement* conducted an online survey, which found that 65 per cent of primary school teachers and 72 per cent of secondary school teachers were planning to vote Labour. In both groups, the percentage of Tory voters failed to reach even double figures. A similar survey of UK university staff in 2019 for *Times Higher Education* found 54 per cent planning to vote for Labour, 23 per cent for the Liberal Democrats and just 8 per cent for the Conservatives.

It is not, of course, the private political opinions of teachers and lecturers that concern Mr Roberts. It is the culture created within institutions dominated by a single way of thinking, and the influence that may have on students' political leanings. After the 2019 Conservative victory, Twitter account @ElectionMapsUK released an analysis showing how Britain's political map would have looked if only 18–24-year-olds had voted. Instead of Mr Johnson's 80-seat victory, it found that Labour would have secured a staggering majority of 438 seats.

Labour's commanding lead in the youth vote is a relatively recent phenomenon, only really opening up in such a striking fashion in the last two general elections of 2017 and 2019. It may be a short-term effect caused by Corbynmania and fears over Brexit. But as John Gray put it in his *New Statesman* essay,

> their support for Corbyn is also a by-product of beliefs and values they have absorbed at school and university. According to the progressive ideology that has been instilled in them, the West is uniquely malignant, the ultimate source of injustice and oppression throughout the world, and Western power and values essentially illegitimate.

And for Conservative strategists, this is too unnerving a prospect to ignore. If these young Labour voters do not change their views as they age, future elections will be unwinnable for the Tories. In such a climate, it is also no surprise to find opposition parties voicing their wholehearted enthusiasm for reforming the voting age downward.

Many more examples could be drawn from across our major institutions. In the established Church, the BBC and the civil service, 'progressive' ideals of a more equal society through government intervention are in the ascendant and set the terms of debate. The political gossip site *Guido Fawkes* recently investigated the relative funding and airtime of groups lobbying for increased state spending and of those in favour of less spending and more free-market solutions. The groups arguing for higher spending had 40 times more funding and 37 times more staff. Over a week, they were quoted by the national media six times more often.

But to really understand the concerns of Conservatives about a Gramscian takeover, we must look beyond the nexus of Labour support among faculty and students, or even the ideological leanings of other major institutions, to the behaviour of the Conservative party itself.

In 2019, the late Sir Roger Scruton, then Britain's most famous living philosopher, was accused of racism and drummed out of a government appointment by a Twitter hate mob, whipped up in the wake of an interview for the *New Statesman*. George Eaton, the magazine's deputy editor, who conducted the interview, posted a photo of himself on Instagram, which he later deleted, in which he was drinking from a bottle of champagne. The accompanying caption said: 'The feeling when you get right-wing racist and homophobe Roger Scruton sacked as a Tory government adviser.'

Later, the full transcript of the interview revealed that Sir Roger had been the victim of selective quotation on Twitter. The *New Statesman* apologised, and he was reappointed as co-chair of the Building Better, Building Beautiful Commission, which he had been leading before the media storm.

The damage, however, had been done. What mattered was not that the *New Statesman* had gone after a Tory. Such an aggressive attack was uncharacteristic of the magazine under

Jason Cowley's editorship, which has tended toward more thoughtful contributions, like the essay by John Gray cited above; but it was, after all, still the house journal of the intellectual left. What the Scruton scandal laid bare was the ineffectiveness – and even complicity – of Conservatives as the attack landed.

Within five hours of the accusations being laid against him, Sir Roger was sacked as chairman of the Building Better, Building Beautiful Commission by the Conservative housing minister, James Brokenshire. In the intervening hours, prominent Conservatives had thrown Sir Roger under the bus, using his plight to polish their own anti-racist credentials. Johnny Mercer MP said of his dismissal, 'Let's not take our time.' George Osborne, former chancellor and current editor of the *Evening Standard*, called Scruton's remarks 'bigoted' and also called for his head, asking on Twitter: 'How can Downing Street possibly keep Roger Scruton as a government adviser?' Danny Finkelstein, a Tory lord and *Times* columnist, saw Mr Osborne's tweet, and responded succinctly: 'I agree.'

The Scruton affair was shocking, because it revealed a Conservative party running scared: desperate to prove that it measured up to cultural standards set by the left, and unable to defend even one of its most remarkable minds from a cultural storm whipped up on flimsy evidence. As Sir Roger put it himself in a public statement after the *New Statesman* apologised: 'I am grateful to the *New Statesman* at least for this, that these distressing events have awoken me to the true moral crisis of the Party to which, despite everything, I still belong.'

The crisis was not just moral, however, but cultural. Tests of our character and moral courage arrive in moments of weakness, not of strength; and this extraordinary episode revealed the weakness of political power in the face of a cultural attack. When even a sitting government and a former chancellor fail to stand up for their own allies, it reveals more than lack of character – it reveals a cultural force able to humiliate and put to the test the highest in the land.

It was gutless of party grandees not to stand by a man who had devoted his life to arguing for their view of the world. It also proved that it is not enough for Conservatives to win elections. A culture hostile to conservatism had the power to force the government and its fellow travellers either to risk their own ruin or to sacrifice one of the best friends they had. After such a moment, the idea that there is an ongoing culture war in this country seems foolish. A Britain where a Conservative government gives over Roger Scruton to the mob is a Britain where conservatism has already been culturally defeated.

Sir Roger's death earlier this year provided an opportunity for Mr Johnson to set out his stall as a Tory prime minister who would act very differently. His response to the news was to tweet: 'RIP Sir Roger Scruton. We have lost the greatest modern conservative thinker – who not only had the guts to say what he thought but said it beautifully.' But as we have seen, such defiance is also accompanied by defensiveness, as in Mr Johnson's unwillingness to put senior officials up for certain BBC interviews. And his policy programme has already been criticised for the concessions it makes to the left's free-spending, interventionist agenda on issues ranging from the environment to the NHS.

The test of the new Conservative government will not be the content of its tweets, but whether it can actually carry off some conservative policies. The experience of life under Theresa May's premiership does not offer hope. In particular, a much less well-publicised event in 2019 makes plain the scale of cultural defeat that Mr Johnson's new government is facing. That event was the publication of new statutory guidance on relationships and sex education by the Department for Education. Again, this is a case where the actions of Conservative politicians produced an outcome – here, a change of policy – indistinguishable from that which might have been expected if the government was in the hands of their opponents.

In 2016, Conservative Education Secretary Justine Greening announced that she was considering making sex education compulsory in English schools and it was near the top of her in-tray. Neil Carmichael, the Conservative chair of the Education Select Committee, told the press he was pleased that Ms Greening was 'carefully considering mandating this'.

Despite a few protests as the trial balloon was floated in the press, the policy was not shot down. Instead, there was much approving and eminently reasonable talk of the need to update the old guidance, so that it would be able to take into account new technological issues, such as 'sexting'. By 2017, compulsory lessons on sexual matters had become Conservative policy. Relationship education was to be mandatory in primary schools from the age of four. Sex education was to be mandatory in secondary schools. While parents can still withdraw their children from sex education, schools are expected to do their best to talk them out of doing so, and there is no right to withdraw children from relationship education. The new guidance would apply to all free schools and academies, previously at liberty to go their own way.

Last year, the statutory guidance was published and the reality of this well-meaning policy began to emerge. Among much else, every state school must now punish anyone caught saying that girls and boys might prefer different things. The 2019 guidance states: 'Schools should be alive to issues such as everyday sexism, misogyny, homophobia and *gender stereotypes* and take positive action to build a culture where these are not tolerated, and any occurrences are identified and tackled' (my emphasis). Boys won't be boys, at least in the playground – or else.

The new rule is absurd if its logic is carried through, and we must hope that common sense will save schools from the worst of its mischief-making potential. But the deeper point is not the nature of any particular rule. From now on, the state has been empowered to rule over the intimate instruction of the nation's children – an instruction that will be shaped according to whatever theories the state chooses to endorse, however absurd. Again, when a Conservative administration is the agent that permits such outcomes, the culture war is no longer in contest. It has been lost.

It is hard to know whether the lobbyists and civil servants who pushed this illiberal policy to the top of the secretary of state's in-tray understood the long and shadowy history of forced education on sexual matters by the state. As we will see, the conquest of institutions often happens more by accident than by conspiracy. But the card-carrying Conservatives who let it through evidently neither knew the ambitions of cultural Marxism nor appreciated the simple danger of placing such power in official hands.

In fact, compulsory sex education has been a Marxist dream since at least the early twentieth century: in 1919, the Hungarian communist György Lukács, as deputy commissar for culture, instituted a sex education programme with the aim of overturning so-called bourgeois, Christian sexual morality. Mr Lukács was, along with Mr Gramsci, one of the founding fathers of the idea of cultural Marxism. It is through the influence of the Frankfurt School, to which Mr Lukács was connected in its earliest phase, that cultural Marxism has had such enormous influence in the West. The Frankfurt School's fascination with cultural power – and the politicisation of sex – has led, through the chicanes of post-Cold War history, to a Tory government outlawing the idea that girls and boys aren't the same. It has also produced the Conservatives' current predicament.

And yet the ideas now ascendant in our institutions are not the doctrines of economic revolution that inspired the long march. Socialism – and even communism – have become newly fashionable, despite the millions of lives ground to dust by their long histories of failure. But the ideas occupying our institutions are more concerned with cultural than economic control. These cultural commissars search out thoughtcrimes. They police language, pay gaps and patterns of representation in the workforce. Diversity will be celebrated. The author Ben Cobley has given this new culture of control a name: the 'system of diversity'.

Boris Johnson has won political office, but the long march through our institutions has ended in a triumph for the cultural Marxists. And while the Marxist dream of a socialist economy has been held back, this cultural triumph is still a defeat for conservatism. One of the great challenges of Mr Johnson's premiership – and one of the great questions of the next decade for Britain – is how much this defeat matters, and what to do next. ⌐

CHAPTER TWO

Meet the Blob

Politics is downstream from culture.

Andrew Breitbart

O'Sullivan's First Law: All organisations that are not actually right-wing will over time become left-wing.

John O'Sullivan, *National Review,* 1989

In 1896, conservatives of all classes – and, of just as much note, of both sexes – filled the Royal Opera House for the annual Grand Habitation of the Primrose League. Outside, a line of carriages extended far up the Strand, the heads of the horses decked out with primroses and yellow and purple ribbons. Inside, the auditorium was packed from stage to the highest gallery. Around the balconies, banks of yellow primroses were interspersed by elaborate banners, proudly hung to announce the names of the local habitations that had sent their representatives to this great gathering.

Pressed in among the crowd was the American journalist Mary Krout, whose first-hand account of this extraordinary event was published in 1899, in her book *A Looker On in London.* Ms Krout writes that prizes were awarded to the most successful local groups of loyal conservatives, including the habitations of Newcastle and Oldham. When it was time for the prime minister, Lord Salisbury, to address the crowd, Ms Krout reports that he said the league's power was

> the action of social influence – the influence of men and women on each other, and of men and women in society, meeting each other in private life. Hitherto political action had been largely the effect either of literary productions or speeches on the platform. The

great change which the last fifteen years had introduced was that political opinions were advocated by those who believed in them, not in ostentatious ways, but in the quiet influence of private life. It was a powerful influence because it was multiplied in infinite proportions throughout the length and breadth of the land.

Lord Salisbury was right to be impressed. By the early 1890s, with over a million paid-up members, the Primrose League had more support than the trade union movement. While it placed men and women on an equal footing and appealed across class boundaries, it was unapologetically conservative in outlook. Members swore on their honour and faith to devote their best efforts 'to the maintenance of religion, of the estates of the realm, and of the Imperial Ascendancy of the British Empire'. By 1910, its membership was around 2 million – making it the largest political organisation with an individual membership in British history. On the eve of the Second World War, it could still pack out the Albert Hall.

Contrast this with a very twenty-first-century social movement. In August 2018, teenage climate-change protester Greta Thunberg sat outside the Swedish parliament for two weeks with a handmade sign that read: 'Skolstrejk för klimatet' ('School strike for the climate'). She was refusing to attend school in the run-up to Sweden's general election, in order to draw attention to climate-change policy.

Ms Thunberg's protest made her a celebrity and sparked a mass movement around the world. In 2019, more than 10,000 schoolchildren from across Britain walked out of their lessons to declare a 'climate strike'. Several thousand gathered to protest in London, and crowds of over a thousand were reported in Exeter, Leeds and Oxford, while several other gatherings mustered in the hundreds. Chanting and waving placards such as 'Climate over capitalism', the crowds were exultant and empowered, feeling themselves part of a global movement. Media coverage was friendly; teachers and parents appeared largely supportive. Even Conservative Environment Secretary Michael Gove expressed his support for the strikes.

Whatever the merits of the case for urgent action on climate change, there is nothing conservative in the idea of 'climate emergency', which seeks to push democratic norms and reasonable discussion aside to get its way – in this case, demanding overwhelming economic and political change on the basis of popular agitation by children. Yet today, our cultural institutions line up behind the idea of young people playing truant to demonstrate for radical changes to the industrial economy. By contrast, mainstream support for the kind of positive and unashamed conservatism of the Primrose League, never mind on such a mass scale, has become unthinkable. The simple idea of ringing Big Ben to celebrate Brexit (a cause which, of the major parties, only the Conservatives now back) caused a storm of protest and led ministers to retreat to avoid accusations of 'triumphalism'. The minting of the Brexit-themed 50 pence coin was immediately mocked and criticised by prominent Remain-supporting individuals like Lord Adonis and Alastair Campbell.

Indeed, figures on the left are happy to announce publicly that they do not even want to spend time in the same room as a Tory, let alone kiss one. Reflecting in January on her electoral defeat, the former Labour MP Laura Pidcock, notorious for her publicly avowed antipathy to anyone who supports the Conservatives, said: 'I don't miss having to look, in the same room, at the Tories every single day.' Today, conservatism is the one exception to the general rule of tolerance above all else: young people are comfortable posting 'No Tories!' in their adverts for flatshares or dating app profiles, but 'No Lefties!' is rarely, if ever, seen. It is another sign that Conservatives no longer control cultural territory, even if they have won an election.

In 2020, the Primrose League is not just a historical curiosity, but a vital touchstone for Britain's new prime minister, as he confronts what (at times) appears to be an entire establishment hostile to his agenda – for the league is both a reminder of what has been lost and perhaps a sign of future possibility. The Primrose League was founded in honour of Benjamin Disraeli (the primrose was said to be his favourite flower), who as Conservative leader and prime minister built a winning coalition that embraced both the patriotic working class and the wealthy landed classes. Historian David Starkey has suggested – including in his 2019 Smith Lecture for the New Culture Forum – that Boris Johnson has the potential to govern as a neo-Disraelian prime minister. Can Mr Johnson weave the working-class voters he has won from a Labour uncomfortable with patriotism into the fabric of a genuinely popular Conservative party? Could a new commitment to Queen and Country revive the level of cultural acceptance and celebration that the league achieved for its commitment to God and Empire?

To do so, Mr Johnson must understand what cultural forces stand in his way. And the answer begins with institutions.

Institutions matter, because they are powerful, enduring and outside the usual political process of a democracy. Centralising institutions and placing them in the hands of the state does not limit this effect. Instead, it only increases institutions' potential for capture and creates a more powerful tool for anyone who succeeds. The power to shape an institution's agenda is a kind of power without term limits or accountability, and it can be immense. Those with an interest in power have always known this. The very phrase 'culture war' comes from the German *Kulturkampf* of the late nineteenth century – a fight between the Prussian state and the Catholic Church for control of educational appointments. Both sides understood how much was at stake. The control of educational institutions has always been a key battlefield in the culture war, because it offers the chance to shape the minds of entire generations.

At around the same time as the *Kulturkampf*, another war for institutional control was being waged in the schools of England and Wales. Research by Professor James Tooley reveals that many of the early proponents of state control of education in the run-up to the 1870 Education Act had very particular ideas about the kind of schooling they wanted to impose, and the kind they wanted to stop. These reformers sought to take control of existing schools (which were already widespread), bringing those institutions under the authority of the state, in order to impose their vision of 'moral betterment' by ensuring the right kind of religious education in the classroom. Ordinary parents were more interested in seeing their children learn the three Rs. But institutional control was wrested from parents by those who felt indoctrination into socially correct norms to be more important. These were social conservatives; but they failed to realise that the institutional power they craved might, in the future, be turned to serve very different ideological aims.

And while state monopolies are especially prone to institutional capture, private enterprise can also suffer from the same problem. In 1970, the Nobel Prize-winning economist Milton Friedman wrote a startling essay for the *New York Times Magazine*. Bold at the time, it now reads as almost unthinkable heresy. It is remembered for his invocation of what came to be known as the 'Friedman doctrine': that a company's only social responsibility should be to increase its profits. In an age when corporate social responsibility (CSR) updates are an expected part of every annual report, few now agree. Everyone forgets, however, why Mr Friedman feared the alternative as 'fundamentally subversive'. He saw that any company that started spending money on 'social responsibility' would be handing that budget over to serve the agendas of the left:

> What it amounts to is an assertion that those who favour the taxes and expenditures in question have failed to persuade a majority of their fellow citizens to be of like mind and that they are seeking to attain by undemocratic procedures what they cannot attain by democratic procedures.

Today's 'woke' corporations, enforcing the latest politically correct doctrines internally and promoting politically fashionable causes externally would have horrified Mr Friedman, but he would not have been surprised.

Few have explained better the thrill of terror that anyone of a conservative inclination should feel at the sight of a powerful institution than the political commentator and former speechwriter to Mrs Thatcher, John O'Sullivan. He proposed his First Law, quoted at the start of this chapter, in 1989: 'All organisations that are not actually right-wing will over time become left-wing.' It was a playful remark, and remarkably pessimistic, given that it was delivered in the year Soviet communism began its collapse. The last 30 years, however, have borne out the truth of O'Sullivan's Law, and it was not formulated without reason. Mr O'Sullivan's point was that the ideas of the left had become widespread in the culture. He then noted the Iron Law of Oligarchy, formulated in 1911 by the sociologist Robert Michels. This states that organisations inevitably become captured by a self-serving elite at odds with those organisations' own founding principles. O'Sullivan's twist was to observe that in the late-twentieth-century West, such capture would naturally tilt organisations to the left, as the permanent officials steadily advance their own views ahead of the institution's original design.

The logic of O'Sullivan's Law applies even more to institutions that actively attract individuals with left-wing views, and so it can help to explain the particular ease with which our educational institutions get captured by the left. More generally, while even private businesses are not immune, taxpayer-funded institutions and non-profit-making bodies like charities and foundations are particularly vulnerable. The economist and social theorist Thomas Sowell gave a succinct but telling reason why, in his 1997 article 'The Survival of the Left': 'The most fundamental fact about the ideas of the political left is that they do not work. Therefore we should not be surprised to find the left concentrated in institutions where ideas do not have to work to survive.' He pointed out that the left's domination of college campuses had a telling exception: any field where decisive tests prevented empty theorising, such as science, mathematics – and athletics.

The control of a single institution offers a huge and enduring source of cultural power, with little or no check on how it is used. Worse yet, institutions over time seem to have a natural tendency to drift leftward, like unmoored boats in a strong current. And some of the institutions with the most cultural power, like schools, are especially prone to drift. All this would be bad enough. But what happens when such institutions come together? A loosely affiliated network of institutions captured for the same worldview is another beast altogether.

The cultural forces that encouraged the copycat climate strikers are an instructive case. Setting aside the rise to fame of Greta Thunberg herself, consider what was required for the school climate strike to succeed. An event that seemed to be spontaneous relied beneath the surface on informal support, not just from one but from a wide range of institutions.

First, the movement needs friendly media coverage. The BBC makes this easier, with its extraordinary dominance of the UK's news-viewing audience and its strong line against climate-change sceptics, such as the Global Warming Policy Foundation. Then it helps to have support from the school system. To begin with, as we have already seen, the teaching profession is preponderantly staffed by those who sympathise with causes of the left. And this may be further accentuated by a more pronounced leftward skew in the institutions that train teachers. That general sympathy is then reinforced by the curriculum. Fierce wars continue to rage over the exact level of compulsory climate-change education. In 2013, when Michael Gove was education secretary, he was accused of limiting the amount of attention the curriculum paid to climate change; he was forced to issue a rebuttal and to stress how much attention students were required to pay to the subject. The degree of lobbying is a reflection of the power of institutional control at stake – here in the form of the power to shape young minds by shaping the curriculum.

Already we can start to see the intersecting power of a number of different institutions: the BBC; schools; teacher training; the officials who oversee the national curriculum. Each of these institutions can have significant individual power if it falls to a particular cause. But when they all do, their agendas merge into a faceless but almost irresistible force. This amorphous, loosely coupled collection of likeminded institutions is a formidable opponent. It does not need to rise to the level of conspiracy to exert a powerful influence in favour of its worldview. And its vague and slippery form is almost impossible to attack.

Meet 'the Blob'.

Michael Gove made the Blob famous when he used it to describe the forces stacked against his education reforms in 2013, sparking loud protests from the educational establishment. The phrase originated in the 1980s, when US Education Secretary William Bennett used it to describe the high-cost, low-output bureaucracy of America's publicly funded schools. But in relation to the wholesale institutional capture of the British education system, it appears to have been first used by the late Chris Woodhead, who was chief inspector of schools in the 1990s, under John Major's government. Mr Woodhead included the phrase in his 2002 bestseller *Class War,* having encountered its vivid use in Robert Holland's essay 'Institutional Roadblocks to Reform', published in America in 2001.

While the phrase is sometimes assumed to be a reference to the 1958 B-movie starring Steve McQueen, in which the titular Blob is an alien, in fact it fits better with the superior 1988 remake. In this (far scarier) version, the Blob is a government-created monster left over from the Cold War that must be defeated by a small group of social rebels. In the words of the trailer: 'If it had a mind, you could reason with it. If it had a body, you could shoot it. If it had a heart, you could kill it.' As Mr Woodhead himself explained, the Blob 'captures the inert mindlessness and sullen, rubbery resistance of the professors and quangocrats and officials and consultants who make up the educational establishment'. Mr Woodhead may have made it notorious, but he was not the first to experience this insubstantial monster. George Walden was appointed as an education minister in the 1980s and, as he reminisced for the *Telegraph* in 2009, a friend told him at the time that reforming education 'was like trying to disperse a fog with a hand grenade: after the flash and the explosion, the fog creeps back'.

For a classic example of the Blob in action, consider the media storm in 2014, when Mr Gove decided not to reappoint as chair of the Ofsted board Lady Morgan of Huyton. Lady Morgan, a lifelong Labour activist, had been one of Tony Blair's closest and longest-serving advisers for a decade. She was actually appointed to the Ofsted board by David Cameron's coalition government. Nonetheless, when the decision was made not to renew her appointment, Lady Morgan made it a story about Tory bias. She appeared on the BBC's *Today* programme to say how it was 'extremely worrying' that the Conservatives were failing to reappoint their ideological opponents to key non-governmental roles. As a result, close Tory allies and donors who had been in line to replace Lady Morgan – David Ross and Theodore Agnew – were sidelined. The compromise candidate, businessman David Hoare, was then driven out two years later, after some ill-advised comments about the Isle of Wight.

Undemocratic, undefinable, near-impossible to pin down or stop. That's the Blob. And now consider that instead of being confined to education, the monster has oozed through all our key institutions, growing in scope and power, while remaining almost undetectable. In 2014, former Environment Secretary Owen Paterson warned of a 'green blob' of lobbyists limiting the options for government policy on the environment. But it was the battle to enact the decision of the Brexit referendum that left many observers convinced that something larger and far more dangerous was at work. Not just a local monster, making particular sectors impossible to reform, but a leviathan that had engulfed every institution in its path. At the start of this year, editor of the *Sunday Telegraph* Allister Heath wrote, assessing Mr Johnson's prospects, '[I]t's No 10 v the Blob, and only one side will be left standing.' His column concluded: 'we shall soon find out whether Johnsonism stands a chance, or whether it will be gradually suffocated by a monolithic left-liberal, anti-democratic Blob convinced that it is the real government of Britain'.

How did we end up here? The next chapters will follow the tangled history of the left's long march to the heart of Britain's institutions, and its transformation from economic to cultural revolution. It is not a tale of conspiracy, but a mixture of active subversion, misadventure and unexpected outcomes for every side. In institution after institution, O'Sullivan's Law has worked itself out, with a series of unlikely assistants. The results have not been what the hard left wanted. The best intentions of some of those who fought back have, at times, made matters worse. The result is now impossible to ignore.

In December 2004, after 121 years, the Primrose League was finally wound up and its last assets donated to the Conservative party. Michael Howard and Liam Fox received a cheque for

£70,000 from Lord Mowbray, but otherwise the moment was barely noticed. Promoting a conservative culture had become little more than a historical curiosity. Tony Blair was well into his second term. A very different set of ideals had taken root.

CHAPTER THREE

The 'Culture Industry' Industry

It is not the consciousness of men that determines their existence, but their social existence that determines their consciousness.

Karl Marx, Preface, *A Contribution to the Critique of Political Economy*, 1859

Look, I probably should have told you this before, but you see ... well ... insanity runs in my family ... It practically gallops.

Arsenic and Old Lace, 1944

A remarkable film was released in 1944: Powell and Pressburger's *A Canterbury Tale*. Beautiful, odd and utterly original, it manages to combine a touching depiction of the encounter between American servicemen and the rural English, between a war-scarred present and the deep time of English history, and between everyday moments and the sacred. It is one of a kind – one of my favourite films – and yet it was not alone that year. Even as the Second World War continued, in 1944 the Anglo-American film industry managed to produce a roster of now-classic movies: *Double Indemnity*, *Arsenic and Old Lace*, *To Have and Have Not*. The great writer-director Preston Sturges managed to release not one but two: not only the outrageous *Miracle of Morgan's Creek,* but also his satire of military heroism *Hail, The Conquering Hero.*

These films were masterpieces of popular art, across a wide spectrum of genres and moods. Some were playful and irreverent; some were more serious. All were enlivening. Who would have entertained the idea that these polymorphous products of a free society were part of a problem that needed to be fixed?

But in 1944, a text called *Philosophische Fragmente* had been published in New York and was circulating among likeminded intellectuals. Its authors looked on works of popular entertainment with an attitude of despair, shading into horror. Its 500 mimeographed copies were the antithesis of Hollywood mass distribution, and yet the ideas were destined to shake Western culture. In three years' time, the revised text, by Max Horkheimer and Theodor Adorno, would be published as *Dialektik der Aufklärung – The Dialectic of Enlightenment*.

One chapter in particular was called 'The Culture Industry: Enlightenment as Mass Deception'. It proclaimed: 'Films, radio and magazines make up a system which is uniform as a whole and in every part.' This should have been disproved by a passing glance at contemporary popular cinema, but Mr Horkheimer and Mr Adorno were too serious to see what was staring them in the face. Instead, they looked so deeply that they could see nothing except their own worst fears.

The culture industry, they argued, was part of a system that was keeping the capitalist masses docile, by feeding them indistinguishable, unchallenging pap:

> Not only are the hit songs, stars, and soap operas
> cyclically recurrent and rigidly invariable types, but the
> specific content of the entertainment itself is derived
> from them and only appears to change. The details are
> interchangeable. The short interval sequence which
> was effective in a hit song, the hero's momentary fall
> from grace (which he accepts as good sport), the rough
> treatment which the beloved gets from the male star,
> the latter's rugged defiance of the spoilt heiress, are, like
> all the other details, ready-made clichés to be slotted in
> anywhere; they never do anything more than fulfil the
> purpose allotted them in the overall plan. Their whole
> raison d'être is to confirm it by being its constituent parts.
> As soon as the film begins, it is quite clear how it will
> end, and who will be rewarded, punished, or forgotten.
> In light music, once the trained ear has heard the first
> notes of the hit song, it can guess what is coming and

feel flattered when it does come. The average length of the short story has to be rigidly adhered to. Even gags, effects, and jokes are calculated like the setting in which they are placed. They are the responsibility of special experts and their narrow range makes it easy for them to be apportioned in the office.

The result of this allegedly formulaic culture was, the authors argued, toxic. Political and economic revolution was being waylaid by cultural institutions that were insufficiently radical. And the result was not just a population that was unwilling to sell itself into communist slavery – it was one small step from coming out and waving swastika flags for Hitler: 'the bourgeois … is already virtually a Nazi'.

Who were the men telling America, even as it was still fighting a great and terrible war against fascism and militarism, that it was as bad as the enemies on whose destruction it had expended so much blood and treasure? Who had the gall, even as the country's mass entertainment industry was producing numerous original works of art that remain fresh after more than 75 years, to pronounce it a mere machine for stupefaction?

The authors of 'The Culture Industry' were sophisticated and erudite refugees from Europe, deeply engaged with the creative arts, and friends with the powerful. Far from being a distant commentator, Mr Adorno spent time in Hollywood with Charlie Chaplin and Fritz Lang, even as he wrote his critique. But these brilliant refugees were committed Marxists, with a grim suspicion of the capitalist world. They had come by their profound pessimism honestly, as Jews observing the rise of Hitler at first hand. Now, though, they made the mistake of seeing the society around them in America as a similar obstacle on the road to communist happiness.

One crucial idea developed in 'The Culture Industry' was that the forms of commercial culture were actively instilling a sense of obedience in the mass population. As the authors saw it, such an encouragement of passivity only prepared the ground for a fascist leader to emerge and start giving orders.

The inherent tendency of radio is to make the speaker's word, the false commandment, absolute. A recommendation becomes an order. The recommendation of the same commodities under different proprietary names, the scientifically based praise of the laxative in the announcer's smooth voice between the overture from *La Traviata* and that from *Rienzi* is the only thing that no longer works, because of its silliness. One day the edict of production, the actual advertisement (whose actuality is at present concealed by the pretence of a choice) can turn into the open command of the Führer.

Certain ideas are so odd that only an intellectual could think of them. The notion that running advertisements for competing products was a kind of training ground for Nazis deserves some kind of special award for its foolishness. Had it been expressed more briefly and in plain language, even fellow intellectuals would surely not have taken it so seriously. Were there really no significant differences between the radio broadcasts of President Roosevelt or Winston Churchill and those of Adolf Hitler, because the impact of the medium itself made all political broadcasts a form of irresistible command? But these scholars saw hidden influence everywhere, and perceived the ordinary citizen as little more than an easily manipulated pawn in the great game of ideological power. Rescued from the monster of Nazism, they had brought the ideas of the Frankfurt School with them. As the Second World War ended, the cultural fight was just beginning.

But the origins of the Frankfurt School and cultural Marxism lie a few decades earlier, in the fallout of the First World War and the disillusionment of Europe's communists, as their hope faded that a world revolution would flourish in the wreckage.

Karl Marx and Friedrich Engels published *The Communist Manifesto* in 1848, in anticipation of a revolution in Germany, which failed. *Das Kapital* volume 1 followed in 1867. Half a century passed before the October Revolution of 1917 saw Russia become the first state where communists successfully seized power. But Russia was an agrarian economy, not an industrial one like Britain and Germany. And it was the industrial powers which Marx had regarded as vulnerable to revolution from below. For believers in Marxism, it was a frustrating puzzle. The shocking dislocation of the First World War left empires shattered and buried many conventional pieties in the mud of Flanders. It seemed like the natural point at which history must at last turn against the capitalists of the industrial West and give them their long overdue comeuppance. But once again, the revolution was postponed.

Nor were the inter-war years simply a return to the same old stalemate. A new dream of control was emerging in Europe: fascism. This rival revolutionary force, inspired in part by the mobilisation of state power in the Great War, began to take hold in its aftermath. The communists were left struggling to understand not just the longevity of capitalism, but the successful rise of a rival totalitarian agenda.

This was the context in which Antonio Gramsci would formulate his own ideas about the importance of culture to break the deadlock. In 1921, after a successful career as a journalist and commentator for socialist newspapers, his interest became not just theoretical but practical. Mr Gramsci helped to found the Communist Party of Italy, just as Mussolini's fascists were coming to power. He was imprisoned in 1926, and at his trial the prosecutor declared: 'For twenty years we must stop this brain from functioning.'

The fascists had their way, although not quite as they would have hoped. Mr Gramsci was locked up for 11 years, and during that time his health was destroyed. He died in 1937, just before his release. However, despite his illness, Mr Gramsci used his time in prison to write extensively on the theory of revolution and to develop his idea of the power of cultural hegemony. Thanks to his imprisonment, the world outside was not aware of how fiercely the lifelong revolutionary's brain was still functioning. The contents of his prison notebooks went unknown and unpublished for decades. In 1944, their re-emergence was still a few years away, and the first translations into English would not be published until 1957.

But the world that drove Mr Gramsci to develop his theories was that of inter-war Europe. He was facing two questions that would also dog the Frankfurt School. First, why hasn't the inevitable revolution that Marx predicted taken place? And second, how can we bring communism not just to Russia, but to Western nations?

As a journalist in 1916, Mr Gramsci was already troubled by these themes. And although he diverged from conventional Marxism, it was in the ideas of Marx that he already found the seed of an answer. Marx believed that there was no such thing as a fixed human nature, but rather that people were shaped like clay by their socio-economic conditions. Later, Mr Gramsci would take a step further and make the case for hegemonic culture as a shaping force, not just economic and political conditions. But as he wrote in one column from this early period: 'Man is above all else mind, consciousness – that is, he is a product of history, not of nature. There is no other way of explaining why socialism has not come into existence already.' It was an idea that chimed with the thesis of 'The Culture Industry': potential revolutionaries are indoctrinated out of their ability to see the communist light.

György Lukács, too, whom we met in a previous chapter, was also rapt with frustrated longing for a communist future. After his brief political career in 1919 as people's commissar for education and culture in Hungary, he was still happy to tear down 'bourgeois culture' to get there. He believed that revolutionaries would create new values of their own, but that first they needed to torch those that already existed: 'A worldwide overturning of values cannot take place without the annihilation of the old values.' In 1969, looking back on his younger days, he wrote: 'I saw the revolutionary destruction of society as the one and only solution.'

In search of others who shared his view of the world, Lukács gravitated in the 1920s to the fledgling Frankfurt School – the Institut für Sozialforschung (Institute for Social Research, or IfS). Although he would not be involved for long, it would develop many of the ideas he cared about. The founder was Felix Weil, the well-off son of a grain merchant, who had become a passionate student of Marxism. In 1922, Mr Weil organised a week-long conference, attended by Mr Lukács and dedicated to synthesising various strands of Marxist thought. It was a success, and in 1923 the IfS was founded.

Because Mr Lukács was a member of the communist party, he could not join the IfS when it became an official part of Frankfurt University. And his affiliations caught him from both directions, for the heterodox Marxism that was a specialism of the IfS was not in line with the official doctrine of his own party. Indeed, the leader who would shape the institute into its most influential form, Mr Horkheimer, did not even describe himself as a Marxist.

Resistant to categorisation, insidious, the Frankfurt School was on its way: an academic hothouse that was willing to think the unthinkable and reconceive Marxist theory, and whose intellectuals were also willing to imagine that the best way to serve Western civilisation might be to destroy it. Six years later, in 1930, Max Horkheimer became IfS director. He would hire not just Theodor Adorno, with whom he would write *The Dialectic of Enlightenment*, but also a whole raft of dangerous minds, including the psychoanalyst Erich Fromm and Herbert Marcuse, who would become a superstar of the 1960s counterculture.

Mr Fromm had left the school by the end of the 1930s, but the presence of a psychoanalyst is worth noting, since it highlights one of the curious hybrid strands of Marxist thought that would remain important to the Frankfurt worldview. The combination of Freud and Marx allowed a connection between political liberation and sexual awakening that was to prove an explosive mix in the 1960s, especially in the hands of Mr Marcuse.

Wilhelm Reich, not part of the Frankfurt milieu, was another pioneer of Freudomarxist explanations, albeit an exceptionally eccentric one. His 1933 book *The Mass Psychology of Fascism* blamed Germans' sexual repression for their acceptance of Hitler as Führer. Like Mr Lukács, he found the official communist party unimpressed by his original approach: he was thrown out for his pains. But he persisted in his heresy, self-publishing his ideas. Three years later, he published *Die Sexualität im Kulturkampf* (*Sexuality in the Culture War*; it was later retitled *The Sexual Revolution*). Under threat from the Nazis, Mr Reich took his seductive ideas to America in 1939, where he built a considerable following by promoting and selling special boxes designed to accumulate 'orgone', a sex energy he claimed to have discovered, before the Food and Drug Administration prosecuted him for fraud.

Nonetheless, Mr Reich's quackery did not keep his ideas from influencing a generation of American intellectuals and writers, including Norman Mailer and Saul Bellow. It was a sign that exciting, countercultural ideas from Europe would find fertile soil in post-war America, however nonsensical they were.

The Frankfurt School followed a similar path. Its members, too, had sought refuge from the Nazis: the school moved to New York in 1935, becoming part of Columbia University and bringing its members into the mainstream of American academia. Mr Adorno and Mr Horkheimer moved to Los Angeles in the 1940s, where they would complete *The Dialectic of Enlightenment*, casting their own patch of pessimistic shadow under the brilliant glare of the Californian sunshine.

The Frankfurt scholars had joined the world of American universities, and they found it hungry for the radical ideas they brought with them. In time, the power of Freudomarxist explanations would re-emerge and would help to reach a far wider audience, as we shall see later. But from the beginning, the cultural Marxists contributed a far less sexy, but no less insidious, idea: critical theory.

This philosophy of suspicion and negation was pioneered by Mr Horkheimer in the 1930s, and became the signature method of the Frankfurt School. As he wrote of the approach in 1937 in 'Traditionelle und Kritische Theorie' ('Traditional and Critical Theory'):

> [I]t is suspicious of the very categories of better, useful, appropriate, productive, and valuable, as these are understood in the present order … the critical attitude of which we are speaking is wholly distrustful of the rules of conduct with which society as presently constituted provides each of its members.

Shaped by both the intellectual pessimism and the revolutionary intent of the Frankfurt scholars, critical theory embraced a new role for the academic: not as neutral and objective enquirer, but as a necessarily partial critic of the status quo. This criticism, as Mr Horkheimer said, was not piecemeal or directed at amelioration of the existing system. It was an attitude of rejection of the totality of capitalist society. Critical theory did not simply seek to attack the capitalist order, but to replace it. Later in the same essay, Mr Horkheimer writes that the critical theorist forms 'a dynamic unity with the oppressed class, so that his presentation of societal contradictions is not merely an expression of the concrete historical situation but also a force within it to stimulate change'. He also described critical theory as 'the kind of theory which is an element in action leading to new social forms'.

The idea of the academic as a necessarily partial activist would have a profound influence on Western universities. Spreading through the humanities and social sciences, critical theory would gain wide currency. This was critical theory in a broader sense than the strict version promoted by the Frankfurt School. Yet it still maintained its commitment to academia as a means to political emancipation – and emancipation was code for awakening others to leftist thought, and the clearing out of existing social, economic and political realities. While parents, employers and politicians worked to send more and more children to university, in the hope of improving their lives, deepening their skills and enriching their cultural understanding, the university itself was changing and setting its own sights on the new generation of students.

Out of a terror of proto-fascist indoctrination, Mr Horkheimer introduced the Western academy to the idea that indoctrination of its brightest and best against the existing order was the only responsible course. Remarkably, eight decades later, critical theory is still at the cutting edge of cultural change. Today's feminists complain about 'the patriarchy', and critical race theorists argue that 'white supremacy' should be understood not as membership of a hate group, but as a term which describes the very structure of our white majority society.

We suffer, we are told now (as then), not from acute problems that can be tackled one by one, but from a chronic and incurable sickness that has infected every aspect of the way we live. And while today's cultural revolutionaries are often less interested in building a socialist economy as an alternative, those who are continue to lurk on the sidelines, waiting for their opportunity. In Britain, that was evident in the hard-left Labour manifesto of Jeremy Corbyn and John McDonnell and the provocateurs of Novara Media: Ash 'I'm literally a communist' Sarkar and Aaron Bastani, author of *Fully Automated Luxury Communism*, published in 2019.

As it fought to secure victory over totalitarian fascism, the United States welcomed a group of brilliant minds, twisted by the failure of communism. They believed that the regime that had rescued them was just a few steps down the road from turning Nazi, and bent their brilliance to the task of Western revolution. In 1944, the long march began.

CHAPTER FOUR

Wolves in Sheep's Clothing

… intellects vast and cool and unsympathetic, regarded this earth with envious eyes, and slowly and surely drew their plans against us.

H.G. Wells, *The War of the Worlds*, 1898

Very few institutions in modern society have found ways of protecting themselves against small groups – well-organized, completely unscrupulous, indifferent to the well-being of their fellows and above all with no coherent and ultimately realizable aim – who set out to destroy them.

Bernard Levin, *The Times*, 3 October 1975

In the Britain of 1945, a different kind of long march had reached its destination. A landslide election defeat for Winston Churchill's Conservatives brought in a Labour government, its benches in parliament packed with 229 members of the Fabian Society – 58 per cent of Labour MPs were members, including many ministers. Labour's winning manifesto had been written by a Fabian, and much of the seismic reform that would follow, including the foundation of the National Health Service, had first been proposed in Fabian tracts.

Seventy years earlier, the Fabian Society had been created with the aim of transforming Britain into a socialist society without the need for violent revolution. It appealed not to the workers in the manner of traditional Marxist groups, but to the intellectual middle class. Its name – and strategy – came from the Roman general, Quintus Fabius Maximus Verrucosus, known as 'Cunctator' ('the delayer'). In the late third century BC, Fabius used delaying tactics against the Carthaginians in the Second Punic War to great effect. First, he bought Rome time to recover its strength, and then he waged a slow war of attrition, refusing to risk his forces in decisive battles and steadily weakening his opponents.

The Fabian strategy was a slow and patient one; but it was also committed to decisive action when the time came. The Fabian Society's first pamphlet announced:

> For the right moment you must wait, as Fabius did most
> patiently, when warring against Hannibal, though many
> censured his delays; but when the time comes you
> must strike hard, as Fabius did, or your waiting will be
> in vain, and fruitless.

In the 1940s, the covers of the society's tracts were decorated with a tortoise raising its front leg like a fist, above the motto: 'When I strike I strike hard.' In 1945, the Fabian moment, long prepared for, had arrived.

The Fabians were successful because they were able to be patient, take a long-term view and develop support for their ideas. They were also masters of exploiting the power of institutions.

As we have seen, institutions have huge political significance, in large part because of their ability to endure, and not only to preserve their culture but to pass on their values across human generations. Such institutions are well suited to long-term strategies; for when won over to a cause, they will continue to fight for it long after their creators are dead.

Committed to the slow accumulation of political influence, the Fabians from the outset sought the control of institutions that could help their cause. One key tactic was to infiltrate their ideas into established bodies that were not socialist. The society called it 'permeation'.

The Fabians have always had a reputation for secrecy – a reputation that they have not always been at pains to dispel. A stained-glass window, now installed at the London School of Economics, was made in 1910 to celebrate the society by Fabian member Caroline Townshend. It was presented to the playwright George Bernard Shaw, who, along with Beatrice and Sidney Webb, was one of the founders of the society. The window features many famous faces associated with the Fabians, including the author H.G. Wells, who had a stormy and brief membership. It also depicts Mr Shaw and Mr Webb hammering the world into shape beneath a crest decorated with a wolf in sheep's clothing.

Looking back in 1928, already happy with the society's achievements, Mr Shaw wrote in *The Intelligent Woman's Guide to Socialism and Capitalism* that:

> The Fabian Society succeeded because it addressed itself to its own class in order that it might set about doing the necessary brain work of planning Socialist organization for all classes, meanwhile accepting, instead of trying to supersede, the existing political organizations which it intended to permeate with the Socialist conception of human society.

The tactic of permeation was adopted by the Fabians from the 1880s, and it reflected the Fabian belief in the effectiveness of persuasion, rather than the violence proposed by revolutionary Marxists. The Fabians set out to sell their ideas, piece by piece, to groups that other socialists would have considered irredeemable. In 1915, the political scientist Ernest Barker described the Fabian approach in his book *Political Thought in England from Herbert Spencer to the Present Day*:

> An intellectual circle has sought to permeate all classes, from the top to the bottom, with a common opinion in favour of social control of socially created values. Resolved to permeate all classes, it has not preached class-consciousness; it has worked as much with and through Liberal 'capitalists' as with and through Labour representatives. Resolved gradually to permeate, it has not been revolutionary: it has relied on the slow growth of opinion.

Permeating white-labelled versions of socialist ideas into existing institutions and across party lines, the Fabians were developing their own form of a long march toward political power. However, the Fabian approach was committed to rational argument, and its adherents were generally open about their socialist beliefs and aims. Their gradualist strategy was advertised in their name and their tortoise logo. The power of slow growth is that, even if you acknowledge your ultimate goal is to transform society, each step you take towards that transformation is so small that it looks innocuous and is hard to resist.

But the Fabians did not simply seek to hijack existing institutions: they also understood the power of building new, sympathetic institutions of their own. The Fabian Society itself is the proof: now in its 136th year, it remains an important think tank. While 1945 was its high-water mark, it also played a significant role in the rise of New Labour to power in the 1990s. After the 1997 election, once again there were more than 200 Fabians on the Labour benches. When Chancellor Gordon Brown made his momentous announcement declaring the independence of the Bank of England, he was picking up an idea that Ed Balls had proposed five years earlier in a Fabian pamphlet. As a publisher and promoter, the Fabian Society developed a community of ideas that has changed Britain and the world, and may well continue to do so.

Nor was the Fabian Society content with establishing its own institutional power. It was also instrumental, alongside the unions, in the creation of the Labour party, forging the political force that would enact its policy proposals in 1945. And two founding Fabians, Beatrice and Sidney Webb, with the help and support of the society and its donors, created both the London School of Economics and the *New Statesman*.

But mention of the Webbs brings us to an altogether darker kind of cultural warfare. For the Webbs, having spent many years as public faces of the respectable, gradualist left, ended their lives as passionate Stalinists, willing to ignore the evidence of hideous crimes, in order to defend Soviet communism and promote it as the system of the future. As such, they were an early part of the vast secret network of misinformation and cultural propaganda that the Soviets threaded across the Western world and which would operate until the end of the Cold War.

In 1935, the Webbs, now retired and well into their sixties, published *Soviet Communism: A New Civilisation?* Widely recognised today as a shameless work of pro-Soviet propaganda, on its release it was a bestseller, read at all levels of society. The Liberal politician Sir Ernest Simon was swept away by the book, devoting his holiday in the Lake District to consuming it rather than walking. As Sir Ernest wrote to the Webbs:

> Thirty years ago you started me on my public career
> by the Minority Report [on reform of the Poor Laws,
> headed by Mrs Webb and published in 1909, said to have
> planted the seed that grew into the welfare state]. I don't
> yet know what you have done to me this time! But it is
> certainly the most exciting, stimulating and important
> book I ever read.

The second edition, two years later, was published without a question mark in the title.

In 1940, George Orwell wrote that 'there is something wrong with a regime that needs a pyramid of corpses every few years … All people who are morally sound have known since about 1931 that the Russian regime stinks.' But the Webbs travelled to the Soviet Union in 1932 and, they said, 'fell in love' with what they found. Evidence of Soviet brutality continued to grow, not least in the shape of the *Holodomor*, Stalin's deliberate starvation-murder of millions of Ukrainians in 1932–33 for political ends. But the Webbs died in the 1940s, still his unrepentant supporters.

For decades, the Soviets actively sought out dupes and fellow travellers who would spread lies about the glories of communism into the West. In his *Double Lives: Stalin, Willi Munzenberg and the Seduction of the Intellectuals* – a history of the Soviet system of cultural subversion – Stephen Koch explains why the Western intelligentsia proved so rich a hunting ground for communism's propagandists:

The adversary culture is a branch of the middle class;
usually its most vigorous intellectual and artistic wing.
It is drawn, albeit ambivalently, to radicalism; radicalism
is part of its vision of freedom and truth … Elite youth
can be best discerned in the *quality* of their protest. They
are likely to carry the presumptions of that protest into
middle age, and into authority. Catch that protest in its
school days. Develop it properly. Deepen it, convince
it, frighten it, blackmail it, network it. Then you will
have forged the unseen 'revolutionary' bond between
Bohemia and power.

Soviet spies are often remembered today as those who
passed on state secrets, especially military ones. But the cultural
side was just as important. Guy Burgess, one of Britain's most
notorious spies and a member of the Cambridge Five, worked
for the BBC before he joined the Foreign Office. Mr Koch writes:

Burgess advanced spectacularly through the Bloomsbury
networks; he was soon the most influential political
producer in the entire BBC, where he introduced
Soviet propagandists and fellow travellers wholesale.
This naturally included Anthony Blunt, whose many
appearances at the BBC were most useful in his rise.

But such spies had to keep their affiliation secret, in order to
make their way into the top ranks of society. And the communists
were no more popular among the poor. As the historian Robert
Service says in his book *Comrades!*, communism in Western
Europe 'held next to no appeal to the imagination of the industrial
working class in whose name it had been invented'.

With the Second World War over and the Cold War under way,
open support for communism had become suspect. Britain's
two communist MPs both lost their seats in 1950, and no official
communist candidate would ever win again. Flagrant support
for communism could also limit options to co-opt universities:
Mr Service gives the example in *Comrades!* of Andrew Rothstein,
lecturer in Russian History at London University's School of

Slavonic and East European Studies, whose contract was not renewed in 1950 because of 'his party membership and militancy'. In November 1950, the House of Commons held an adjournment debate addressing fears of communist infiltration in the teaching profession.

However, there was one vital area where leftist sympathisers, perhaps even some with close ties to Moscow, did gain a foothold: the institutions of teacher training. The parliamentary debate of 1950 cited particular concerns that emergency training colleges short of staff had been infiltrated by communists at the end of the Second World War, although with little hard evidence. Matters became far worse after 1973, when the government made it compulsory for teachers in state secondary schools to have completed an accredited training course, either a Postgraduate Certificate in Education or a Bachelor of Education degree.

Inevitably, any institution for teacher training is a prime target for ideological capture. That such training was made compulsory in the early 1970s was fateful timing. The social sciences were then deeply influenced by Marxist ideas, made newly acceptable by the New Left (on which see the following chapter). In 1989, the Hillgate Group published a pamphlet entitled *Learning to Teach*. It gives examples of some of the results. Madan Sarup, a lecturer in education at Goldsmith's College, London, and an avowed Marxist-Leninist, wrote a book based on a compulsory course for trainee teachers called *The Politics of Multiracial Education*. He wrote that teachers 'should be developers of "critical consciousness" amongst their communities. They must link up with other teachers, not only in their staff room and teachers' centres, but in unions and political parties.' Members of ethnic minorities who seek self-improvement are dismissed as 'a class of collaborators who justify the ways of a capitalist state to the blacks and are engaged in domestic neo-colonialism'.

Brighton Polytechnic's teacher training was a particularly notorious example, brought to public attention by Malcolm Pearson in the late 1980s. The education department included staff members like Clive Griggs, who was a senior lecturer and taught a course on the influence education has on the fabric of society, and was also the education correspondent for the socialist *Tribune*. An article in *The Spectator* at the time by Michael Trend reported on the course outlines for Brighton's teachers-to-be, stuffed with phrases like 'the theory of patriarchy' and 'education for class equality'. Mr Trend summarised: 'Here, then, are almost all the tired, old assumptions of the left, especially those on "anti-sexism" and "anti-racism", dressed in the whole panoply of relativism and social engineering.'

But teacher training was unusual: it was hard to monitor and its effects slow to percolate into society. It was also reliant, in what would prove a wider trend, on a new kind of leftist politics, not on the sort of pro-Soviet agitprop that the Webbs had produced.

During the Cold War, the Soviets themselves understood that operating through apparently independent institutions would be vital. In 1951, the Communist Party of Great Britain claimed independence from Moscow and dropped the dictatorship of the proletariat from its stated objectives. According to Mr Service, Stalin vetted and amended the draft personally.

Even such pretences of independence could not save communist political groups in the West from irrelevance, and after the late 1960s they descended into the kind of internecine squabbles immortalised in *The Life of Brian*'s 'Judean People's Front' scene. But other groups hid their affiliation, and had more luck.

The Militant Tendency, which infiltrated its members into the Labour party and pretended not to exist as a separate organisation, took over Liverpool City Council in the 1980s. As Mr Service writes, 'the key to its effectiveness was clandestine parasitism'. However, gaining political power proved a mistake. The Militants were a disaster in office, burning through the council budget. Eventually, the banks called time on the ballooning deficit and taxis had to be hired to deliver redundancy notices to city employees. After this debacle, seized on with glee by Margaret Thatcher, Neil Kinnock had the authority to see the Militants expelled from the party, and their influence shrivelled accordingly.

The peace movement was more successful. Respectably free of any communist labels and not at risk of having its views tested by reality, these campaigners proved a valuable cultural force to help undermine Western military resolve. Funnelling money to several groups via the Assistance Fund for Communist Parties and Movements of the Left, Moscow helped to keep the protests going. In Brian Crozier's memoir *Free Agent: The Unseen War, 1941–1991*, he wrote: 'Ever since its creation in 1948, the World Peace Council had been one of the most successful of the Soviet-controlled international fronts.'

On the battlefront of nuclear disarmament, the culture war and the arms race met. It was not enough for the West to be physically capable of winning a war if its own people did not want to fight. As Mr Service says: 'The Cold War remained a struggle for Western minds as much as a competition in weapons delivery.'

But the successes were intermittent and never decisive. For all its subterfuge, Moscow's secret war failed to gain the West's sympathy. The horrors of Soviet life, even glimpsed through a smokescreen of propaganda, were unavoidable. The Webbs did not have the final word on Stalin. Like the Fabians in the early twentieth century, it would be new and homegrown versions of leftist thought, established in opposition to the authoritarianism of Stalin and the USSR, that would capture Western minds and institutions. The heterodox Marxists of the Frankfurt School, now with a beachhead in the United States, would be at the centre of that revolution.

Meanwhile, the costs of the Soviet disinformation machine continued to climb. In 1991, a Soviet diplomat noted in his diary the anger of the post-communist supporters of Boris Yeltsin over how much money the Kremlin was pouring into these efforts – to so little effect. In 1990, Foreign Minister Eduard Shevardnadze told the Party Congress in Moscow that the ideological fight with the West – a euphemism for the USSR's propaganda machine – had cost 700 billion roubles since 1970. Mr Crozier calculates that this amounts to 'the almost surrealistic average yearly figure of £35 billion for the conduct of the Cold War on the Soviet side'. He adds: 'Ironically this vast expenditure contributed – along with the gigantic defence budgets – to the bankruptcy of the USSR.' ℂ

CHAPTER FIVE

Mao, Marx and Marcuse

… it is Social Democratic garbage to assert that … the whole filthy bunch would allow itself to be infiltrated, to be led around by the nose, to be overpowered, to be intimidated, to be abolished without a struggle. Make it clear that the Revolution will not be an Easter Parade … In order to push the conflict as far as possible, we build up the Red Army.

Red Army Faction, 'Manifesto for Armed Action', 1970

You say you'll change the constitution
Well, you know
We all want to change your head
You tell me it's the institution
Well, you know
You better free your mind instead
But if you go carrying pictures of Chairman Mao
You ain't going to make it with anyone anyhow.

Lyrics to verse three of 'Revolution', The Beatles, 1968

In the summer of 1976, an Air France plane was hijacked in the name of Palestinian liberation. The Airbus A300 was flown to Entebbe in Uganda, where the terrorists were personally welcomed by Idi Amin. Then the passengers were divided into two groups. The majority were released, but all the Jews – just over a hundred people, mostly Israeli – were herded together and kept as hostages. The terrorists announced that if their demands were not met, they would kill the hostages. The Israeli response was a remarkable rescue mission that famously saved most of the passengers' lives and killed all of the hijackers. Two of these, it turned out, were not Palestinian. They were German radicals, part of a movement that had stirred political idealists across the

West. Its most loyal foot soldiers would fight on into the 1990s, justifying their brutality in the name of a socialist dream. But for most of their fellow travellers, that dream lay dead on the bloodstained tarmac at Entebbe. They had wanted to change the world. Their hopes ended in Jew hatred, murder and collusion with a brutal tyrant.

In the 1960s and 1970s, a new revolutionary movement emerged in the West. Repelled by the authoritarian horrors of Soviet communism, it also drew on the Frankfurt School's philosophy of disillusion to see incipient Nazism and stifling cultural control in Western democracies. As a homegrown movement, the New Left found a far more receptive audience than even the best-disguised Soviet propaganda. But its commitment to liberation came with a new enthusiasm for political violence.

In 2001, Germany's foreign minister, Joschka Fischer, came under fire after old pictures emerged of his radical youth, which placed him close to violent street protests in Frankfurt in 1973. To explain his political journey, Mr Fischer told *Stern* magazine of his horrified realisation in 1976 that he had known one of the Entebbe hijackers. Willi Böse and Mr Fischer had moved in the same radical circles in Frankfurt, where Mr Böse was known for his knack at playing moustache-twirling capitalist villains in street theatre agitprop. Mr Fischer explained that his revulsion at what happened in Entebbe shocked him out of any sympathy for the violent left. As Paul Berman writes in his *New Republic* essay 'The Passion of Joschka Fischer', his story was that of an entire generation.

In Britain, an essay by the historian E.P. Thompson for the *New Reasoner* in May 1959 announced the arrival of the New Left as an intellectual force. A year later, the *New Reasoner* would merge with *Universities and Left Review* to create the *New Left Review*, which would be the house organ in Britain for these ideas. Like many others drawn to the New Left, Mr Thompson had been a card-carrying communist and remained a committed Marxist; but in the wake of the Soviet suppression of the Hungarian Uprising in 1956, he broke from the party and sought new expressions for his revolutionary beliefs.

In his 1959 essay, entitled simply 'The New Left', Mr Thompson identifies a younger generation that is hostile to existing institutions, whether of left or right:

> These institutions enshrine and perpetuate attitudes which have their origin in a pre-war context; they appear, to the post-war generation, as institutions set apart from and above them. This is notably the case with the British Labour Party … They see restriction where their fathers saw mutual support. And the young socialist today is not only concerned with changing the direction of Labour Party policy; he is hostile to its integration with the rest of the Establishment, hostile to the party bureaucracy, hostile to the 'game political', hostile to the machine itself.

Introducing a theme that would be central to the New Left's programme of action, Mr Thompson also identified the importance of cultural influence:

> The work of changing people's values and attitudes and the summoning up of aspirations to further change by means of Utopian critiques of existing society, remains as much a duty of socialists as the conquest and maintenance of working-class power.

Such shifting of values and attitudes went hand in hand with an interest in controlling the mechanisms of communication, and he noted specifically in the British context that:

> The problem presents itself as one of constructing (however painfully slow the process may seem – though steady progress is being made) an alternative 'cultural apparatus', firmly in the hands of the New Left, a cultural apparatus which by-passes the mass media and the party machinery, and which opens up direct channels between significant socialist groupings inside and outside the labour movement.

Yet here already we can observe a tension in Mr Thompson's thought that would reveal itself in darker ways as the movement at large matured. His vision is anti-authoritarian, standing in deliberate contrast to the nightmare of mass obedience which he saw as defining both the Soviet and the Western system. As in the quote above, Mr Thompson argues not for a new 'enlightened' despotism where his acolytes command the mass media, but for a New Left that seeks to smash monopolies of thought and develop alternatives to mass media. As he puts it: 'We have seen enough of a socialism … where "culture" is a means of social control directed by the Establishments.' At the same time, Mr Thompson was a revolutionary, committed to imposing a new mode of life on society at large. The hope of a socialism that offered liberation without either violence or indoctrination was naïve, and both these tactics would in practice come to define the activists of the New Left.

In America, at the same time, a disciple of the Frankfurt School had begun to take its ideas mainstream. The German scholar Herbert Marcuse was to become the intellectual godfather of New Left counterculture. In 1955, his book *Eros and Civilization* had returned to the connection between sexuality and political revolution, which we have already encountered in the activism of György Lukács and the Frankfurt School's interest in combining Freudianism and Marxism. Just as the post-war generation began to come of age, Mr Marcuse offered intellectual cover for sexual indulgence. It was an irresistible message, and the idea that the path to a higher civilisation freed from repression might lie through a commitment to personal pleasure laid the groundwork for the cultural experimentation that would define the Sixties.

But it was in 1965, with the publication of *One-Dimensional Man* that Mr Marcuse reached a new level of fame. The book sold hundreds of thousands of copies. Drawing on the characteristic cultural pessimism of the Frankfurt School, it presented consumer society as a comfortable cage that needed to be rejected in the name of human freedom. Echoing Mr Thompson's concerns, it sets itself against mass indoctrination, but struggles to escape metaphors of elimination that imply less-than-liberal tactics: 'Intellectual freedom would mean the restoration of individual thought now absorbed by mass communication and indoctrination, abolition of "public opinion" together with its makers.'

A far more sinister glimpse of where these contradictions would lead appears in an essay by Mr Marcuse that was published two years later and called 'Repressive Tolerance'. This makes the case that, in the face of cultural domination, revolutionary ideas can only get a fair hearing by intolerance toward the dominant ideology. Or, in plain terms: 'Liberating tolerance, then, would mean intolerance against movements from the Right and toleration of movements from the Left.' In a postscript which he added when the essay was republished in 1968, Mr Marcuse makes his position clear:

> The tolerance which is the life element, the token of a
> free society, will never be the gift of the powers that be;
> it can … only be won in the sustained effort of radical
> minorities … militantly intolerant and disobedient to
> the rules of behavior which tolerate destruction and
> suppression.

By 1968, such arguments for militant intolerance and disobedience had already opened the gates to political violence. With people being told that their societies were authoritarian nightmares threatening to destroy civilisation itself, and that the system's oppression was overwhelming and inescapable, it was hardly a surprise. On the streets of Paris, where it seemed that student rebels, in concert with a widespread strike, might bring down the government, the slogan of 'Mao, Marx and Marcuse' captured the mix of armed and intellectual rebellion.

But in Europe, another intellectual's influence was being felt, as the works of Antonio Gramsci escaped their obscurity, following his long imprisonment, and returned to shape a new generation of Marxists.

While independent of the Frankfurt School's work, Mr Gramsci's *Prison Notebooks* offer a related model of how cultural control – in Mr Gramsci's thought, hegemony – could stand in the way of socialist revolution. But Mr Gramsci's theory also offered a vision that was less despairing, and which would offer revolutionaries an alternative path without recourse to violence.

The crucial distinction Mr Gramsci made was between a 'war of position' and a 'war of manoeuvre'. The war of manoeuvre was the conventional idea of a final revolutionary offensive that would impose a socialist system. But for Mr Gramsci, it had to be preceded by the war of position, which sought to shape the cultural environment of a society to make it receptive to the possibility of revolution. The war of position, despite the military metaphor, was a long ideological struggle.

In this long struggle, Mr Gramsci saw a vital role for the 'organic intellectual', who understood the power of social systems as an organic, hegemonic whole, and who worked for a particular class interest. The war for position, he argued in the *Prison Notebooks*, required winning over conventional intellectuals in their various fields, but also the creation of organic intellectuals devoted to the interests of the revolution:

> One of the most important characteristics of any group
> that is developing towards dominance is its struggle
> to assimilate and conquer 'ideologically' the traditional
> intellectuals, but their assimilation and conquest is made
> quicker and more efficacious the more the group in
> question succeeds in simultaneously elaborating its
> own organic intellectuals.

The ideas of Mr Gramsci became especially influential among the Eurocommunist movement of the 1970s, in which the communist parties across a number of Western European countries broke with Soviet communism and sought their own approach to revolution. And in Germany, where Mr Fischer was spending his radical youth and the New Left's weakness for violence had begun to spiral toward nightmare, Mr Gramsci's ideas gave birth to a new alternative: the idea of a 'long march through the institutions' was finally named.

As the Sixties ended, and the exhilaration of 1968 faded, the New Left became tainted with its connection to violence. In

1968, the Beatles' song 'Revolution' was an early marker of the counterculture's discomfort with the reality of pitched street battles, and its preference for sexual revolution. Lennon's lyrics made a straightforward statement to the band's legions of fans: you won't get laid by talking up Maoism. But even as the mainstream appeal of direct action fell away, the New Left's militants were becoming more radical than ever. Even Mr Marcuse at times found himself at odds with the revolutionaries' new course. A 1970 profile in *Playboy* magazine by Michael Horowitz recounts a telling confrontation between the scholarly Mr Marcuse and anti-intellectual students who were ready to reject the 'white man's' courses in favour of ignorance. As Mr Horowitz wrote: 'The kids thrill to phrases like "undermine the foundations of the system" … while the professor would have them temper such excitement with the reading of *Das Kapital* in the original German.'

In Britain, this militancy would emerge as a violent, but short-lived, fringe. The Angry Brigade was responsible for 25 bombings between 1970 and 1972, primarily aimed at causing property damage. In Germany, things were far worse. In 1970, the Red Army Faction, which would become notorious as the Baader–Meinhof Gang, published its manifesto – quoted at the start of this chapter – which was unashamed in its commitment to violence, announcing: 'Let the armed resistance begin!' Over the next 28 years, it would be responsible for bombings, murders, kidnapping and robberies that left more than 30 people dead. This was the strand of the New Left that produced Entebbe, and ultimately so horrified Mr Fischer. Among the hijackers' demands in 1976 was the release of several members of the Red Army Faction imprisoned in West Germany.

From the beginning, even many fellow radicals were appalled by these tactics. They seemed a betrayal of the New Left's commitment to human liberation and of its rejection of the politics of force and brutality. In 1977, Mr Marcuse himself wrote an article for *Die Zeit* – published in English by the *New German Critique* as 'Murder is Not a Political Weapon' – condemning terrorism in West Germany:

Those representatives of capital whom the terrorists have
chosen as their victims are themselves responsible for
capitalism – just as Hitler and Himmler were responsible
for the concentration camps. This means that the victims
of terror are not innocent – but their guilt can only be
expiated through the abolition of capitalism itself.

These dissenting radicals were still determined to destroy the
society around them, but they needed a more peaceful tactic. It
was formulated by another German radical, Rudi Dutschke. Mr
Dutschke drew on the theories of Mr Gramsci to propose a multi-
decade takeover of society's commanding heights. Drawing on
the history of Chairman Mao's rise to power in China through
military force, he named his strategy 'the long march through the
institutions'. A year before the riots in Paris that came to define
the violent side of the New Left, Rudi Dutschke's portrait was
already on the cover of *Der Spiegel*, in December 1967. The article
inside was titled 'Der lange Marsch'.

Unlike the Red Army Faction, the long march would receive
Mr Marcuse's personal blessing. In a 1971 letter to Mr Dutschke,
reproduced in *Marxism, Revolution and Utopia,* he wrote:
'Let me tell you this: that I regard your notion of the "long march
through the institutions" as the only effective way, now more than
ever.' And in his book *Counterrevolution and Revolt*, published
in 1972, Mr Marcuse would write, approvingly: 'To extend the
base of the student movement, Rudi Dutschke has proposed
the strategy of the *long march through the institutions*: working
against the established institutions while working in them.'

Indeed, as early as the 1970 *Playboy* interview, faced with the
anti-intellectual radicals who wanted to burn everything down,
Mr Marcuse offered a counter-example based on institutional
infiltration. He explained how his students had used protests to
force the University of California into hiring a Marxist economics
professor.

The long march was an improvement on the brutality of
the Red Brigade terrorists and their allies, but both approaches
were born of the same internal contradictions within the New
Left. The movement had begun as a reaction to central control,

committed to breaking up systems of mass indoctrination. But the longing to make its socialist utopia real turned one wing into murderers. It led others to embrace indoctrination: no longer determined to smash oppressive institutions of coercion, they sought instead to capture that power for socialist ends.

As Mr Fischer's rise to the heart of the German political establishment shows, in Germany the long march brought veterans of the New Left to considerable influence. It is also notable that in Mr Fischer's case this came about through the environmental movement and the Green party, which provided a new home for those seeking to radically remake their society.

In Britain, too, the long-march strategy was at work. We have already seen in the previous chapter how some members of the New Left sought to influence teacher training in a radical direction. Perhaps one of the most shocking and well-documented examples of the battle for higher education was that of North London Polytechnic, recounted in *The Rape of Reason*, written by three of the polytechnic's members of staff, Keith Jacka, Caroline Cox and John Marks. Published in 1975, the story of the institution's takeover by radicals was picked up by Bernard Levin in *The Times*, where he wrote a series of three articles on the case. Mr Levin captures the shocking nature of what the book revealed:

> *Rape of Reason* tells, with an astonishing degree of judicious calm, of the planned destruction of an institution of higher education, with the use by the destroyers of physical and psychological intimidation, of totally unscrupulous dishonesty, of violence, theft and vandalism, of obscenity and defamation and of a wide range of literally criminal actions. It tells also of something worse: that is, the resignation and retreat, in the face of this campaign, by those whose undoubted task it was to resist and combat the corruption. And it tells, finally of something worse still: of the way in which the assault was actively aided by some of those who had

the duty of defending free inquiry, intellectual tolerance
and integrity of thought but who instead connived at
the assault on all three and indeed frequently helped to
instigate it.

The events at North London Polytechnic are the long-march
strategy unmasked. While they were unusual in their extremity,
they also show the principles that underpinned its approach
everywhere. To pursue the long march was to be committed
to undemocratic means – Mr Dutschke was very clear from the
beginning that he had no interest in becoming a politician and
standing for election. Its adherents were also absolutists, feeling
nothing but contempt for the culture they sought to overthrow.
And as a result, they felt justified in treating their opponents
as essentially inhuman. Its tactics stopped short of physical
violence, but intimidation and character assassination were
wholly acceptable.

Elements of the New Left's cultural influence would persist,
especially in teacher training. In a report published by the
Institute of Economic Affairs in 1999, Geoffrey Partington writes:

> Although the amount of time available for educational
> theory of any kind was much less in 1997 than 1979, I
> found that the New Left proselytising was as intense as
> ever in some of the remaining areas in which it could
> be practised … Curriculum courses in science and
> mathematics, reading and literacy were as likely to show
> the signs of New Left hegemony as were history or social
> studies.

And yet it was not as an active conspiracy that the long march
would have its greatest impact. More widely, the New Left vision
of a slow-motion cultural revolution offered the radicals of the
Sixties and Seventies a way to move into adult society without
feeling that they had entirely compromised their youthful
principles. Alongside the few consciously attempting to subvert
institutions was an entire generation revolted by violence, but
committed to the principle of social change.

This domesticated radicalism brought beneficial changes: notably around gender roles, homosexual rights and reduced racial discrimination. But it also meant that the New Left's ethos of liberation and its suspicion of capitalist systems became endemic in the wider culture.

In particular, the sexual revolution – always intended by its Marxist promoters as a means to undermine Western society, not to improve it – became permanent. Free love, too, brought many entertaining benefits; but over time, its harvest of divorce and declining marriages steadily undermined the bedrock institution of the family. The consequences are still playing out. On some accounts, the results include the rise of identity politics. The American author Mary Eberstadt argues, in her book *Primal Screams*, that the loss of familial identity has left a generation angry, lost and lonely, desperate to find an answer to who they are and turning to identity politics as a result. As we will see, this latest mutation of revolutionary ideology has now marched to the heights of institutional power. Perhaps the New Left's sexual subversives have had the last laugh after all.

More simply, the default progressivism that the New Left's disillusioned disciples held onto provided the conditions for O'Sullivan's First Law to function. Even without the active conspiracy of Mr Dutschke's heirs, the dynamic of society had shifted decisively towards institutional capture by progressive, rather than conservative ideals.

And yet reality would fight back. The 1970s found Britain weighed down by economic sclerosis, as the spread of socialist ideas corrupted its economic dynamism. With the election of Margaret Thatcher in 1979, there began a new phase in the culture war. 🎧

CHAPTER SIX

The Thatcher Revolution

… tax reform, like other reforms we have introduced, is in the end about changing the very culture of this country.
Nigel Lawson, 'Tax Reform: The Government's Record', 1988

I want us to be a young country again.
Tony Blair, Labour conference speech, 1995

Mid-way through Tony Blair's second term as prime minister, an icon of the New Left expressed his horror at the political landscape that had emerged since the 1970s. Stuart Hall, a leading cultural theorist and founding editor of the *New Left Review*, sensing the emergence of a new counter-revolutionary force, had coined the term 'Thatcherism' even before Mrs Thatcher became prime minister. In 2003, more than a quarter-century later, he felt that Britain was still in the grip of a Gramscian rebellion from the right. An article of his for the *Guardian* was headlined 'New Labour Has Picked Up Where Thatcherism Left Off' and bemoaned the fact that Tony Blair's reforms amounted to a 'new ethos of managerial authoritarianism', planted on top of a firmly Thatcherite view of the world.

For Mr Hall, Mrs Thatcher's rise showed the right, rather than the left, learning from the cultural Marxists and fighting for hegemony. In 1987, he wrote an essay for *Marxism Today* – 'Gramsci and Us' – which explored the theme. It was republished the following year as part of his book *The Hard Road to Renewal: Thatcherism and the Crisis of the Left*. In 'Gramsci and Us', Hall argues that Mrs Thatcher had seized Britain's moment of post-war crisis, and had marshalled policy not to achieve piecemeal improvements, but as part of a programme to transform the culture. Thatcherism's aim, he said, was nothing less than a 'reversal in ordinary common sense':

> Thatcherism's project was to transform the state in order to restructure society: to decentre, to displace, the whole post-war formation; to reverse the political culture which had formed the basis of the political settlement – the historic compromise between labour and capital – which had been in place from 1945 onwards.

It is beyond question that Mrs Thatcher did aim to be a transformational leader (and in many ways succeeded). She needed to be: socialism was tightening its grip on Britain's economy and on its entrepreneurial and individualistic culture. The Thatcher government inherited the collapsing legacy of post-war Fabianism and faced the present danger of Soviet and New Left subversion. The Iron Lady rose to the challenge, with profound, wide-ranging political and economic reforms.

As in the political transformations of the British welfare system in 1945, Thatcherism's ideas had been decades in the making. Richard Cockett's 1995 history, *Thinking the Unthinkable: Think-tanks and the Economic Counter-revolution, 1931–1983,* traces that process in detail. The revival of economic liberalism relied on the work of scholars like Friedrich von Hayek and Milton Friedman. It was also encouraged by think tanks, especially the Institute of Economic Affairs, founded in 1955 and committed, like the Fabians, to fighting a long-term war of ideas. This slow-motion strategy allowed the classical liberals to infiltrate their rival ideas into intellectual circles dominated by socialist assumptions. Having devoted half a century to regaining its lost traction, by the 1980s the individualistic political tradition was ready to make a comeback. As Mr Hall notes, however, this was a political and economic project with cultural goals. For Mrs Thatcher, the revival and reawakening of Britain from the doldrums of the Seventies required economic and political change from above. Individualism was, however, her guiding principle, and as such her larger goals included a moral revival. As she told a Conservative party rally in 1976: 'let us make our vision of a roused, a renewed, and a morally great Britain a reality'.

For Mrs Thatcher, a restructured economy was a means to put in place the incentives for individual betterment – not just financially, but in terms of character and personal virtue. The spread of home ownership would inculcate prudence and responsibility. The ability to keep more of what you earned would inspire diligence. A general bonfire of privilege would allow talent from across society more opportunities to contribute.

In this respect, Mrs Thatcher's achievements fell short of her ambitions. Charles Moore, her biographer, attributes to Peregrine Worsthorne the waspish quip that despite aiming to remake Britain in the image of her father, a strict Methodist, she introduced a culture more in line with her troublesome son, who left the UK amid concerns among senior civil servants that he was exploiting the family name to make money. The journalist and historian Andy Beckett interviewed Norman Tebbit, one of Mrs Thatcher's close political allies, soon after her death in 2013, and Mr Tebbit told him that in hindsight 'our economic reforms led to an individualism in other values, in ways we didn't anticipate'.

Mrs Thatcher sought cultural change through political action. As such, the ideological bias of non-political institutions was not her priority. She did appoint Marmaduke Hussey as chairman of the BBC in 1986, but his major contribution was to improve the organisation's financial management and corporate governance, rather than to police its output. Indeed, the perception of Lord Hussey as Mrs Thatcher's man made it even more important for him to assert the broadcaster's editorial independence from Downing Street. On his appointment, he quashed calls from Mr Tebbit for an investigation into the BBC's 'biased' coverage of America's strikes on Libya. In 1988, the *Today* programme aired 'Thatcherism: The Final Solution', an item implying that Mrs Thatcher would favour legalising drugs in order to kill off unproductive members of society. Furious letters to Lord Hussey from Mrs Thatcher's husband Denis had no effect.

However, Mrs Thatcher's political and economic success did undercut her opponents, even as they remained dominant in education and the arts. In the summer of 1988, the '20 June Group' was founded, in an amateurish effort to formulate some kind of response. Its members were a veritable *Who's Who* of the British cultural elite, including Salman Rushdie, David Hare,

53

John Mortimer, Margaret Drabble and Harold Pinter. According to Caroline Crampton's mini-history of the group for the *New Statesman*, its meetings lingered on until 1992, but without any noticeable impact. More generally, a *Vanity Fair* profile in 1989 commented on the state of cultural dissent: 'Today, the disaffected intelligentsia would say that she has virtually killed off socialism and co-opted the media, that there is no "left" to speak of in Britain.'

That was hardly true. Indeed, it was in an effort to keep the left from commandeering institutions of local politics that Mrs Thatcher would pursue a strategy of reducing such institutions' power. The Greater London Council under 'Red' Ken Livingstone was a very public source of opposition, until its abolition in 1986. Further policies sought to limit the spending power of local councils and the influence of local education authorities.

Often, this approach restored power to individuals in the form of greater choice. The sale of council homes and the creation of grant-maintained schools are examples of this. But reform was from the centre, over the heads of local government bodies; and while it weakened the political influence of those institutions, it also pushed power towards the centre. Grant-maintained schools were taken out of local authority control and funded directly from Whitehall. Ironically, this strategy at times ended up creating a far greater prize for whoever grasped the national levers of power. It would prove a fateful gift to the political left when it returned in the form of New Labour.

Perhaps the most striking example of this is the creation of the National Curriculum in the Education Reform Act of 1988. For Mrs Thatcher, this was intended as a form of light-touch regulation, guaranteeing basic and uncontroversial standards. Instead, it grew into a significant institutional apparatus that laid out in detail what schools should teach. As such, Mrs Thatcher unwittingly created a new tool by which her opponents could engage in cultural warfare. In 2002, former Chief Inspector of Schools Chris Woodhead, a former enthusiast of the National Curriculum, wrote: 'The prospect now is of a curriculum that enshrines the evils it was meant to defeat, and that is not a good scenario. The rats will continue to gnaw away. It is a lost cause.'

Mr Woodhead served as chief inspector under the governments of both John Major and Mr Blair. While the election of New Labour in 1997 was a political earthquake, it was also, as Mr Hall appreciated, a form of continuity. Mrs Thatcher had established a new hegemonic common sense, reinforced by the practical outcomes of her reforms. Two decades on from the crises of the Seventies, Britain in the Nineties was prosperous, optimistic and creative. There was a new-found and politically hard-won respect for the effectiveness and morality of market solutions based on individual choice. Socialism was no longer cool.

New Labour was the result: a reinvention of the Labour party that accepted many of Mrs Thatcher's ideas about market efficiency, but sought a 'Third Way', in which goals of state-supported social equality could be aligned with market mechanisms. Mr Blair also saw that the social conservatism of Mrs Thatcher had failed to take hold; he offered a political identity for those who appreciated economic reality, but also held socially liberal views.

The difference between Thatcherism and its Blairite heirs lay in the natural inclinations of their political worldviews. Mrs Thatcher's approach, which Mr Hall dubbed 'reactionary modernisation', combined economic change with a promise to restore the national greatness of the past. Mr Blair offered instead a wholehearted progressivism that looked forward to a new and better future, and treated the past as a problem from which it offered an escape route. New Labour's language was technocratic. Its ministers were photographed in front of shiny new buildings and with fashionable, creative artists. The Department of National Heritage became the Department for Culture, Media and Sport.

Along with an acceptance of the economic lessons of Thatcherism, New Labour embraced its legacy of wielding central power in the name of national renewal. Many of these initiatives are still playing out, a decade after New Labour left office. And while the party's constitutional reforms and tight management of the press are well known, other innovations have received less attention or less credit for their political impact. For example, at the end of 2019, the figures for university attendance in 2017–18 were released, showing that 50.2 per cent of people under 30 were at university. This was the first time that Mr Blair's target of 50 per cent of the population attending university – announced in 1999 – had been achieved.

Sending at least half the population to university was, from the outset, considered by many conservative critics to be an unwise target. In 2002, Mr Woodhead wrote that the consequences of such a policy of expansion would be

> dire, for the thousands of students who will find themselves locked into three years of sub-degree study that is unlikely to bring any real intellectual satisfaction and may well not lead to worthwhile employment;
> … dire for us all, in that the survival of a society that understands what it is to participate in civilized and humane conversation depends upon the preservation of universities that are worthy of the name.

In practice, this target has driven a generation of young people into debt, often for degrees of questionable market value. At the same time, it has done little to improve access by students from the poorest communities to the very best universities. And yet the target remains. The policy was fuelled by New Labour's usual blind faith that any unintended consequences could be avoided by managerial wizardry. It ignored common sense, which said that the salary premiums earned by a small pool of graduates would have to drop when the supply of graduates, many with lower-tier degrees, were added to the mix.

Even as a social engineering project, Mr Blair's revolution in higher education has failed. The Russell Group, comprising Britain's elite universities, has seen little change (and in some cases recent declines) in the proportion of disadvantaged students being admitted. In 2014, 50 students on free school meals were admitted to Oxford and Cambridge. In 2007, it had been only five fewer.

Meanwhile, the state of higher education is parlous. A blistering attack on the dumbed-down university sector, written at the end of 2019 by Mary Harrington for the *UnHerd* website, concludes that students are 'graduating in ever greater numbers with ever less valuable degrees'. The latest figures (released in February 2020) show that men who study creative arts subjects at university lose out over a lifetime to the tune of £100,000 compared to their peers who go straight into the workplace. For women, studying creative arts or languages has no benefit at all in terms of future salary. Improved earnings are by no means the be-all and end-all in education; but many could fairly feel misled by the government's relentless promotion of degrees as valuable, even while its policies devalued their currency. Given the levels of student debt accumulated by university attendees, the policy seems at best cruel, and at worst a kind of financial mis-selling. Educational and social ramifications aside, this policy has incidentally guaranteed that half of the population will be exposed in early adulthood to environments where the politics of the left are dominant. The consequences have been politically meaningful.

For proof of that, consider the work of the economic historian Thomas Piketty. Mr Piketty is more famous for his book *Capital*, but in 2018 he published a paper called 'Brahmin Left vs Merchant Right', which explores trends in political affiliation for the United States, France and Britain. His findings for Britain matched those elsewhere: 'high education voters now strongly support Labour', with this trend emerging over the 2000s and 2010s. Mr Piketty's paper is focused on revealing this trend, rather than explaining it. However, he does point to the expansion of education as a plausible cause. But whatever the pattern of causation, the timing of Britain's surge in university attendance coincided with a surge in left-leaning attitudes among graduates. Thanks to Mr Blair's policy, far more individuals were affected by this leftward drift than would otherwise have been the case. And while New Labour itself represented a moderate form of leftism, that does not seem to be the case on campus. Instead, both here and in other countries, like the United States, a climate of increasingly aggressive policing of speech appears to have taken hold, with cases of 'no-platform' activism shouting down speakers from the right.

Mr Piketty also discusses the possible effect of increased immigration and globalisation: the better-educated and wealthy elites are in favour of these, while those on the periphery – those who have suffered more social and economic disruption – are opposed. This is plausible enough in Britain, where recent mass immigration was a conscious choice by Mr Blair's government – a choice whose effects were experienced very differently by upper and lower economic classes. Net migration when Mr Blair came to office stood at 47,000 a year; under his premiership, this figure quadrupled to over 200,000, and by 2005 had hit 320,000. There is much to recommend immigration, and Britain has always been a nation open to new migrants. But this shift was on a scale that only an intellectual could think would have no political consequences.

Given that the new arrivals tended to vote Labour, it has been suggested by some that Mr Blair's administration saw a chance to bolster its support base. However, the tight geographical clustering of new immigrants limits the electoral impact, and makes that theory unlikely (or at least unsuccessful on a national scale). The sheer volume of the new arrivals appears to have been a shock even to the planners, and in the long run, of course, it has had quite the opposite effect, disillusioning traditional Labour voters. But certainly, in the early years, New Labour's ideologues had no incentive to change course when they saw what they had unleashed.

A glimpse of the ideological basis for this historic shift came in a notorious article written for the *Evening Standard* in 2009 by Mr Blair's former speechwriter, Andrew Neather. It's a nasty and remarkably unaware piece, in which Mr Neather says that without immigrant nannies, you'd have to have a 'fascist' from Burnley or Barking to look after your children. Sensationally, he claimed that, for some of those planning the acceleration of immigration, it was intended to have the side benefit not of importing Labour voters, but of rendering Conservative arguments against multiculturalism out of date: 'to rub the Right's noses in diversity'. He wrote: 'That seemed to me to be a manoeuvre too far.'

Mr Neather also claimed that early drafts of the report from the Performance and Innovation Unit (PIU) that launched the immigration revolution made it clear that 'mass immigration was the way that the Government was going to make the UK truly multicultural'. However, these drafts were later released, and didn't quite live up to this billing: there is no sign of such a plot, although the documents do quote uncritically the Berlin Communique on Progressive Governance, which states, with religious certainty, that 'We are committed to fostering social inclusion and respect for ethnic, cultural and religious diversity, because they make our societies strong, our economies more flexible and promote exchange of ideas and knowledge.' Closer to the historical mark than any sort of full-blown conspiracy is probably Mr Neather's observation that: 'Part by accident, part by design, the Government had created its longed-for immigration boom.'

The report, in both its published and its draft versions, is nonetheless instructive. A classic piece of managerialist double-talk, it is blithe about risk and confident in the ability of technocrats to predict and control the future for the greater good. Rather like an optical illusion which switches before your eyes from duck to rabbit and back again, the report presents the rise of mass immigration as inevitable, something out of the government's hands, before switching seamlessly to declaring its promotion and acceleration as a new priority for government. The report opens with a quote from Tony Blair at Davos: 'We have the chance in this century to achieve an open world, an open economy, and an open global society with unprecedented opportunities for people and business.' To this end, its fourth chapter proposes remaking Home Office Aim 6, which defines the goals of immigration policy. In a telling passage that was deleted from the final published report, the authors argue that the government should eliminate the older goal of trying to strike a balance between social stability and economic growth, because there was simply no need. On their analysis: 'an economically beneficial migration policy will also have positive social impact'.

Supported by revolutions in migration and higher education policy, the growing leftism of Britain's educated class would feed into another tactic that New Labour made distinctively its own: a zeal for managing public appointments. While the practice of giving jobs to political allies was hardly new, New Labour seized upon it with the same discipline and effectiveness with which the media were handled by its spin doctors. Progressive advocates (of which the expanded universities produced an increasingly ample supply) came to dominate and shape the cultures of the unelected institutions that were moulding Britain's future – the quangos (quasi-autonomous non-governmental organisations).

This was not what Mr Blair had promised. The Labour manifesto of 1997 attacked the Conservatives for backing 'unaccountable quangos', and the previous year Mr Blair had told his party conference that they would consign the quango state to 'the dustbin of history'. This complaint had some merit: quangos had flourished under Mrs Thatcher, growing in the 1980s to number more than 2,000. But in office, New Labour's anti-quango rhetoric would change: by 2006, the annual cost of such agencies had topped £167 billion, a breath-taking increase from just over £24 billion in 1998. At the same time, New Labour had embraced the art of appointing friends and cronies to oversee these bodies. Indeed, two years before the New Labour landslide, a proposal was already circulating – written by Labour activist and prominent Fabian Jenny Jeger – to establish a list of Labour-friendly names for public appointments.

As the New Labour project moved into its final years, this process even accelerated. In 2012, *Spectator* editor Fraser Nelson wrote in the *Telegraph* that Mr Brown, in his last two years in government (2008–10), had created a special team at Number 10 dedicated to installing Labour loyalists across public bodies – in order to help preserve the party's political legacy against an incoming Conservative administration. In addition, Mr Nelson pointed to a change at about the same time in the rules surrounding charitable campaigning: in 2008, the Charity Commission for England and Wales revised its guidance on political campaigning to give greater encouragement for charities to intervene in public debate. The new guidance stated: 'The commission's experience is that some charities have been overly cautious, and inclined to self-censor their campaigning activity.' The result was to give more power to left-leaning institutions to influence Britain's political future.

The arrival of a new Conservative prime minister failed to change this pattern. Like Mr Blair before him, David Cameron promised a 'bonfire of the quangos'. This led to some initial cuts, but he failed to stop the quangocracy from continuing its steady expansion. More seriously, he did nothing to end New Labour's takeover of this shadow administration. At the end of Mr Major's government, the majority (57 per cent) of appointees with declared political leanings were Conservative. In 2011–12, after Mr Cameron's election, 76.7 per cent of public appointees with a declared political affiliation were Labour supporters and just 13.8 per cent were Conservatives. Whether Mr Cameron was preoccupied with his policy of 'detoxifying' the Tory brand or was hemmed in by his coalition partner, the Liberal Democrats, the result was striking. The trend has never significantly reversed. Even after a decade of Conservative political leadership, the most recent figures – for 2018–19 – reveal that only a minority (31.6 per cent) of such political appointees were avowed Conservatives, while 47.4 per cent were Labour activists and 10.5 per cent were Liberal Democrats.

The growth of quangos and New Labour's zeal in using the appointment process for its political ends helped to create the opportunity for the left's capture of the quangocracy. However, a report from the Policy Exchange think tank in 2013 – *Reforming Public Appointments*, by Michael Pinto-Duschinsky and Lynne Middleton – noted that the reason 'many more declared Labour supporters have gained appointments also seems to be because more Labour supporters have applied'. Despite efforts over many years by the *ConservativeHome* website and others to encourage more Conservative applications, the imbalance has not changed. The infusion of New Labour supporters after 1997 no doubt helped to ensure that those with a Labour point of view would feel more at home in such a setting. But the tendency also has much to do with the trend identified by Mr Piketty and mentioned earlier, by which the highly educated (from which group the heads of quangos will inevitably be drawn) have become predominantly left leaning over the last 20 years.

The result has been to create a robust, loosely allied network of left-oriented like minds, outside the normal political process, with wide-ranging power over British life. Appointees are also concentrated in London and the South, the primary residence of 40 per cent of the most recent crop of (re)appointees. By contrast, just 2.2 per cent are based in the North East. And the group is profoundly interconnected, with some holding positions on several boards.

This institutional capture has been intensified and made more damaging by another New Labour legacy: the rise of managerialism in the public services. In the Eighties, Conservatism often encouraged the idea that business practices were more efficient than those of taxpayer-funded bureaucracies. But for Mrs Thatcher, this was based on the requirement for businesses to be responsive to the demands of their customers if they wanted to survive. New Labour made the introduction of corporate managerial culture into state-funded institutions an end in itself. The result, lacking the discipline provided by the feedback mechanisms of a true marketplace, was corrupting. In 2007, the blogger Chris Dillow published a book entitled *The End of Politics: New Labour and the Folly of Managerialism*, in which he explored this problem:

> New Labour's preference for business over markets
> shows its managerialist bias – because to any
> managerialist, businesses, with their mission statements
> and their illusions of control, are much more congenial
> than the disruptive anarchic forces of the market.

Managerialism presents itself as an orderly, neutral and universal technique, designed to improve efficiency without reference either to politics or to the particular character of any institution. It is the opposite of the specific, rooted professional cultures that grow up around individual institutions. Indeed, managerialism works by replacing an emergent culture – based on local knowledge and committed to an institution's goals – with generalised approaches and arbitrary targets. In their 2000 textbook *New Managerialism, New Welfare?*, John Clarke, Sharon Gewirtz and Eugene McLaughlin write: 'a central issue in the managerialisation of public services has been the concerted effort to displace or subordinate the claims of professionalism.' A professional culture is one dominated by those who rise from its ranks; managerialism is imposed from without, and its exponents claim to see further by not knowing the system from the inside.

This can lead to improvements, to the extent that the manager's perspective is insightful, and targets are both useful and well measured. But this approach is also inhuman. It denies the importance of institutional culture, the unpredictability of reality, and ignores the ways in which people work around systems that are imposed upon them. Ultimately, managerialism hollows out organisations, separating the management layer from an understanding of the work being done or of its importance.

Healthy institutional cultures organise a community at all levels around the same goal. Managerialism relies on incentives to direct personal ambition. As such, it is vulnerable to those who choose to advance their interests by manipulating the system, rather than accepting it. Goal-less workplaces fall prey to managers who indulge in political game-playing and the artificial manipulation of targets.

Worse yet, behind its neutral façade, managerialism's destruction of professional cultures leaves an empty space that is readily colonised by new and alien ideas. These may be highly partial and even antagonistic to the institution's original goal; but if they serve the interests of the managerial class, they will be preserved and may even take precedence. This is, in fact, another way of stating the mechanisms at work behind O'Sullivan's Law: to the extent that professionalism is replaced with managerialism, institutions will become left wing over time.

Indeed, O'Sullivan's Law has its origin in fears of a rising tide of managerialism. Mr O'Sullivan first encountered Michels' Law of Oligarchy, from which he derived his own Law, in James Burnham's book *The Machiavellians*. Mr Burnham was much exercised by these themes of bureaucratic capture, and two years before had written *The Managerial Revolution*, in which he outlined how managerial ideas might create a new elite that would, for better or worse, dominate the future of capitalism.

Mr Dillow observed something very similar emerging out of New Labour's drive for managerialist efficiency. At its core, managerialism believes that power belongs in the hands of a cognitive elite. Its model of the world is one in which uncertainty can be handled by prediction and control. Managerial experts – and they alone – have the necessary detachment and educated foresight to see what is going to happen and to manage the necessary changes.

Blinded by the idea that he was imitating the efficiency of markets, Mr Blair let a new kind of centralised bureaucracy, dressed in business clothes, off its leash. In Mr Dillow's words:

> Markets are tumultuous, unpredictable and
> uncontrollable processes, which often make fools of
> the most esteemed expert ... Businesses, however,
> are hierarchical bureaucracies and their leaders are
> often more like senior civil servants than buccaneering
> entrepreneurs.

In the wake of New Labour, this was the ideology that captured Britain's top minds. A left-leaning, managerialist Blob oozed inexorably into every corner of power. ⌐

CHAPTER SEVEN

From Political Class to Identity Politics

> The left started the culture war, won it, and now they're roving the country shooting the wounded survivors.
>
> Jon Gabriel (@exjon), Twitter, 19 December 2013

> Contrary to what many people think, the modern liberal-democratic world does not deviate much, in many important aspects, from the world that the communist man dreamed about and that, despite the enormous collective effort, he could not build within the communist institutions. There are differences, to be sure, but they are not so vast that they could be gratefully and unconditionally accepted by someone who has had firsthand experience with both systems, and then moved from one to the other.
>
> Ryszard Legutko, *The Demon in Democracy*, 2016

In 2008, just over a decade into New Labour's time in office, the journalist Peter Oborne identified the rise of a new kind of British elite. No longer marked by class or even political allegiance, these twenty-first-century power-brokers were essentially interchangeable, self-interested and, crucially, insulated from their fellow citizens. The most meaningful gap was no longer between Conservative and Labour: 'The real divide in British public life is no longer between the main political parties, but between the Political Class and the rest.'

Mr Oborne noted that the idea of parliament assembling representatives from across the nation had become a fiction. Politics was a career path, and most of its leading lights followed the same narrow route to power. They generally went to Oxford or Cambridge University, studied Politics, Philosophy and Economics and then plunged straight into the Westminster bubble. Those with a career outside politics still came from a very small set of working backgrounds: PR and advertising, law and journalism.

> The House of Commons is no longer really a cockpit of debate where great conflicts of vision are fought out across the chamber. It has converted instead into a professional group ... comparable to the 'top 10,000' who governed Britain in the nineteenth century before the arrival of universal suffrage.

That connection with journalism and PR was also significant, Mr Oborne argued, because it showed that the media and the political class were unhealthily intertwined. Long-held protocols of debating policy in parliament were replaced with unaccountable media leaks to a tamed press. This new establishment was essentially monocultural. Differences on policy and party membership were superficial and reflected strategic career choices, more than conviction or deeper allegiance.

The idea of a 'political class' struck home, and rapidly entered the language. Mr Oborne's phrase captured a new reality. This unified elite was born of the new common sense on economics created by Mrs Thatcher, but it grew into a monster under the care of New Labour. Its members battened on Britain's ballooning quangocracy, while their outlook tilted steadily to the left. That was due in part to Mr Blair's skill in capturing key appointments for his cronies. It was also a reflection of broader trends, facilitated by the expansion of university attendance, that were edging the educated leftward. The result was more Blairite than Thatcherite. It did not celebrate individualism or past national achievements, but instead looked forward to an increasingly globalised future of government-backed equality. It shared a managerial ethos (while lacking practical managerial experience), believing that it was the place of the elite to set aside accidents of history and impose practical policies that, done right, would both bring prosperity and make society more equal. The need for such policies, not coincidentally, meant an immense transfer of power from individuals – and from civil society and establishment bodies – into the hands of the political class.

This new establishment was self-reinforcing. The managerialists justified their status as a separate, enlightened elite that could ignore the country at large, while having great latitude to interfere in voters' lives for the greater good. Its basic unity nevertheless allowed plenty of room for disagreements over tactics, and the drama of whichever faction was up or down helped to distract from the fundamental lack of variation between party platforms. Heterodox views that broke with that deeper consensus were weeded out early and had little opportunity to gain purchase. The idea of citizenship faded. Those outside the elite were seen instead as consumers.

Arguably for the first time, the dominant worldview among Britain's political and media class was now of the left. However, this was the soft or liberal left, as interpreted through Mr Blair: social liberalism and equality, maintained by government intervention, made efficient by managerialism and paid for by market economics. It appeared to be far from Marxism, cultural or not. Yet, as Mr Oborne revealed, beneath the surface the ideas of Marx were still at work:

> Although communism has enjoyed barely any electoral success in Britain during the last 100 years, its influence has been exceptionally strong among the governing elite, both in politics and other spheres. Two of Tony Blair's most cherished Cabinet ministers, John Reid and Peter Mandelson, had both been active members of Communist organisations … The C[ommunist] P[arty] and the various Marxist factions played a very large part in the education and intellectual construction of numerous members of the Political Class, a phenomenon which cries out for further study.

Mr Oborne notes that the majority of those who ushered in the political class were radical members of the New Left in the 1960s and 1970s. Having set aside Marxist beliefs, they retained 'the organisational doctrines of the far left, and the methodology of centralised control'. This was evident in the elevation of power above all else by the new elite. The critical theorists and Marxist academics that had infected the university system since the 1960s had taught entire generations both that the past was an evil to be escaped from and that formulas about 'rule of law' or 'personal responsibility' were masks for power and stood in the way of personal and political liberation. Like William Roper in Robert Bolt's 1960 play *A Man for All Seasons*, they were willing to 'cut down every law in England' to get after the Devil. Reducing everything to questions of power made the political class careless with matters of legality and even virtue. Ordinary limits had no claim on those who were preparing for the arrival of an inevitable future. In this sense, although they did not seek a communist or even a socialist revolution, their outlook was very Marxist indeed.

The committed cultural Marxists, too, were paying attention. From the Sixties, they had moved towards exploiting divisions around race and gender, rather than those over social class. This gained new traction from the 1990s, with the rise of concerns over 'politically correct' speech, and has spiked again over the last five years as 'identity politics' have come to the fore.

As we saw earlier, on Mary Eberstadt's account, the rise of identity politics is a direct consequence of the sexual revolution and its attack on the institution of the family. However true that is, the tendency was foreseen (and desired) in an influential book published in 1985: *Hegemony and Socialist Strategy* by Ernesto Laclau and Chantal Mouffe, founders of the 'Essex School' of discourse analysis at the University of Essex. The book identifies new opportunities for revolution in protest movements that were not class based:

> the rise of the new feminism, the protest movements of ethnic, national and sexual minorities ... all these imply an extension of social conflictuality to a wide range of areas, which creates the potential ... for an advance towards more free, democratic and egalitarian societies.

Tragically, the politics of identity, diversity and environmental protection could have been tailormade for the new political and media class. Britain's new elite would seize on this prospect with revolutionary zeal, gaining power, curtailing liberty and sowing division. Radical ideas like 'the theory of patriarchy' were once the province of fringe New Left ideologues like those training teachers at Brighton Polytechnic in the 1980s. Through the political class, they would become mainstream.

In a December 1975 article for the journal *Telos*, the sociologist Alvin Gouldner made a telling distinction between revolutionary intellectuals and what he called the 'intelligentsia'. Mr Gouldner's intelligentsia refers to members of the highly educated middle class who inherit and manage the power that comes from the revolutionary ideas of the true intellectuals. As he puts it: 'It is not the proletariat who came to power under "socialism", but first, privileged intellectuals, and, then, privileged intelligentsia.' The intelligentsia lack originality, but gain power by using their technical and managerial skills to expand the ideas of the intellectuals in the name of 'liberation'. At the same time, their lack of imagination cannot escape imposing new forms of social control:

> intelligentsia are technicians who revolutionize culture by exploring the inner space of an established paradigm, neatening it up, fine-tuning it continuously, extending its established principles to new fields, or finding new opportunities of extending practically useful controls … they are both elitists and the bearers of an emancipatory rationality: their rationality enables a critique of the institutionalized forms of domination, but it also contains the seeds of a new form of domination. Their new rationality entails an escape from the constraints of tradition but imposes new constraints on expressivity, imagination, play, and insists on control rather than openness as the key to truth.

The opportunity spotted by Marxist academics to exploit new divisions in society would not have been realised had it not also fitted the agenda of the administrative elite. Britain's new political and media class, committed to both personal advancement and the ideals of state-backed social liberalism, saw nothing to dislike in becoming an intelligentsia with an activist commitment to values of diversity, inclusion and environmental care. It offered them an agenda with a vast 'inner space' that could be explored and expanded into every corner of institutional power. At the same time, it gave a superficially wholesome justification for expanding the scope of their social control and advancing their personal agendas. Consider, for example, the distinctive concerns of this new elite's feminism. Its members are passionate over issues that affect people like them – notably pay and advancement – but have very little time or attention for women being exploited at the other end of the socio-economic scale.

Again, there was no conspiracy. There did not need to be. The wrong idea met the wrong elite at the wrong time. Incentives aligned and the political class cohered around what Ben Cobley, in his book *The Tribe*, has called 'the system of diversity'. And once committed, as an intelligentsia without the imagination to escape their own model, they were trapped. If the result was not social healing, but rather division and resentment, it must be proof that they would be justified in redoubling their efforts and seeking even more control.

Inured to the economic fallacies of Marxism, the elite was not inoculated against its cultural expression. Thatcherism specifically, and the Cold War more generally, had made it more or less common knowledge that seeking equality of economic outcomes was a royal road to tyranny and poverty for all. In the words of Peter Mandelson, one of the architects of New Labour: 'We are intensely relaxed about people getting filthy rich as long as they pay their taxes.' But diversity and inclusion, in particular, presented a disguised form of the same error. Under the mask of liberalism was an illiberal goal: equality of social outcomes. Just like seeking equality of economic outcomes, this cannot be achieved in a complex world without an apparatus of total control. And it cannot be pursued without creating new social divisions. Few realised it was the same Marxist error in a new coat. For the political class, after all, it was a chance to be good and gain power. What could go wrong?

One commentator has recently answered that question by drawing attention to the paradoxical similarities between modern Western democracies and Soviet dictatorship. The socially conservative Polish philosopher and politician Ryszard Legutko is the author of *The Demon in Democracy: Totalitarian Temptations in Free Societies*. Published in 2016, it is quoted at the start of this chapter. Mr Legutko experienced life as a dissident under Soviet-style communism, when he helped to edit a samizdat periodical. He also entered democratic politics in Poland after the collapse of the USSR, serving as education minister in 2007 and becoming a Member of the European Parliament in 2009. Mr Legutko's book explores the curious similarities he found between life in a Soviet-type regime and in the European Union:

> Communism and liberal democracy proved to be all-unifying entities compelling their followers how to think, what to do, how to evaluate events, what to dream, and what language to use. They both had their orthodoxies and their models of an ideal citizen … If the European Parliament is supposed to be the emanation of the spirit of today's liberal democracy, then this spirit is certainly neither good nor beautiful: it has many bad and ugly features, some of which, unfortunately, it shares with the spirit of communism. Even a preliminary contact with the EU institutions allows one to feel a stifling atmosphere typical of a political monopoly.

While Mr Legutko acknowledges that there are profound differences between the two regimes, that today's liberal democratic system 'gives people a lot of freedom and institutional protection' and is 'clearly superior' to its 'criminal' predecessor, he argues that liberal democracy and communism are both regimes 'whose intent is to change reality for the better'. This drives both to narrow the range of acceptable political views and to relentlessly politicise all aspects of everyday life:

> As a result, liberal democracy has become an all-permeating system. There is no, or in any case, cannot

be, any segment of reality that would be arguably and acceptably non-liberal democratic. Whatever happens in school must follow the same pattern as in politics, in politics the same pattern as in art, and in art the same pattern as in the economy: the same problems, the same mechanisms, the same type of thinking, the same language, the same habits. Just as in real socialism, so in real democracy it is difficult to find some nondoctrinal slice of the world, a nondoctrinal image, narrative tone, or thought.

Mr Legutko writes of his experience of Poland before and after 1989, and of the Soviet-like qualities he has observed in the EU's corridors of power. No doubt these correspondences were easier to see from a country where politicians who had held power under communism moved into the new democratic system with surprising ease. And yet his observations speak to life under Britain's new elite as well. As the *Telegraph* columnist Tim Stanley wrote in December 2019, drawing his own comparison to the life under communism and the lies it lived by: 'Britain in 2019 is a liberal fantasyland in which soaps, films, comedies and cartoons tell us everyone is woke, hates Brexit and worships the NHS like a pagan god, except the Tories who are evil.' Indeed, Mr Stanley barely scratches the surface. The uniform invasion of everyday life in Britain by the political obsessions of its new cultural elite is startling. Consider a few examples from the start of 2020.

On 27 January, the Arts Council announced its new 10-year plan called 'Let's Create'. It could have been subtitled: funding the arts for political ends. As the *Telegraph*'s classical music critic Ivan Hewett pointed out, the document outlined four investment principles: inclusivity and relevance; dynamism (in the entrepreneurial, money-raising sense); environmental responsibility; and finally ambition and quality. Only the last suggests a principle connected to artistic merit. As it happens, despite championing 'ambition and quality', the plan explicitly rejects the tradition of valuing high art. The Arts Council doesn't appear to have much time for works of art at all in its next decade, preferring to rename artists 'creative practitioners' and to celebrate the creative process wherever it occurs. As such, Mr Hewett drily observed, even the Arts Council's view of 'quality' 'is something that mysteriously emerges from art when it engages with other things that aren't to do with artistic quality at all'.

On 29 January, longstanding newsreader Alastair Stewart was fired by ITV for tweeting a quote from Shakespeare. The quote from *Measure for Measure* included the word 'ape', and he was accused of racism by the person he was arguing with, ultimately ending his 40-year career. The quote in question was from Isabella's classic call for mercy in an effort to stay her brother's execution. She warns that human ignorance and pride should give pause to those with the power to destroy lives.

On 2 February, Prince William gave a speech at the Bafta awards, in which he expressed his frustration that some of the British film and television awards' shortlists were all male or all white. He added, 'I know that both Pippa [Harris], chair of Bafta, and Amanda [Berry], Bafta CEO, share that frustration and … following this year's nominations, have launched a full and thorough review of the entire awards process.' In 2016, Ms Berry expressed her determination that the awards should become 'as diverse as they possibly can be' and introduced a require-ment – which came into force in 2019 – that in order to be eligible for 'outstanding British film' or 'outstanding debut by a British writer, director or producer', entries would also have to demonstrate their efforts 'to increase the representation of under-represented groups'. In introducing a political as well as an aesthetic standard, Bafta was only running to keep up with its industry. These standards were established by the British Film Institute, and in 2019 they were also adopted by the British Independent Film Awards. Not only do they affect awards, but also funding. The standards apply to the BFI Film Fund, Film4 and BBC Films, making compliance a requirement for the bulk of public funding for film in the UK.

On the same day, the coffee chain Starbucks launched a 'Mermaid Cookie', promising that 50p from each one sold would go to the charity Mermaids to support its transgender helpline.

On 11 February, the environmental think tank Green Alliance held an event entitled 'Countdown to COP26', looking ahead to the UN Climate Change conference to be held in Glasgow in November. Speaking at the event was Nick Bridge, a civil servant from the Foreign Office with the title of special representative for climate change. Almost in passing, Mr Bridge expressed his belief that climate change is the result of 'an economy that functions in a certain way' and his commitment to encouraging 'economic and financial transformation'.

On 12 February, the government announced plans to allow the media regulation quango Ofcom to censor online speech, such as that hosted by social media companies. The powers were to cover not just crimes like child abuse and terrorism, but the broad category of 'cyber-bullying', with companies expected to remove content deemed harmful and to censor and manage content 'with the potential to cause harm'. Ofcom was tasked with drawing up the detailed plans, outside of parliamentary scrutiny, despite the clear risk of politicisation. The same day, its board appointed a new chief executive, Dame Melanie Dawes, whose other roles include being a 'champion for diversity and inclusion' across the civil service.

On the same day, the Church of England's General Synod cut its target for going carbon neutral by 15 years, despite concerns from some attendees that the gesture was likely to be both ineffective and a distraction from its Christian mission. The body also voted to stamp out 'conscious or unconscious racism' and the archbishop of Canterbury announced that the Church was 'deeply institutionally racist'.

On 13 February, the National Theatre's Twitter account tweeted a video clip of a playwright lambasting Conservative policy on the BBC's flagship *Question Time* programme. In the clip, the playwright stated as fact a widely debunked claim which the National Theatre's tweet repeated, saying: '"Austerity has caused the death of over 130,000 human beings in Britain." The moment Francesca Martinez spoke out … She's written a play for us … about the struggle to survive for those who don't fit in.' Shortly afterwards, @nationaltheatre tweeted in reassurance: 'The National Theatre is politically neutral.' Its plans for staging

Ms Martinez's play remained, of course, unchanged.

On 14 February, a High Court judge rebuked the Humberside police for 'disproportionate interference' with free speech, saying: 'We have never lived in an Orwellian society.' The police had visited a man at his workplace over a non-criminal tweet on the issue of transgender rights. However, the judge dismissed the wider complaint against the College of Police guidelines, as he found its aims and objectives sufficient to justify 'the limits it places on free speech'. The guidelines support the recording as a 'hate incident' of any complaint made to the police about an alleged hate crime that is found not to be criminal, 'irrespective of whether there is any evidence' of a hate element. Since 2014, when the rules came into force, more than 120,000 incidents have been logged. Incidents can be shown to prospective employers who require a Disclosure and Barring Service (DBS) check, meaning that those affected could find themselves 'blacklisted' for certain kinds of work on the basis of one unsubstantiated accusation.

On 17 February, the police in Cambridge stood by and refused to make any arrests while the climate revolutionaries known as Extinction Rebellion vandalised the lawn in front of Trinity College and blocked city streets. The radicals, treated as peaceful protesters, had openly declared that their tactics were a form of intimidation, designed to force the overthrow of local democracy and the institution of an unelected 'citizens' assembly' to enforce anti-capitalist dogma.

This list is hardly exhaustive. It offers a snapshot of Britain's educated elite at work today. You cannot turn on the TV, open a newspaper, watch a film or see a play without becoming caught up in the culture war. Enter a church, a school, a university – even a bookshop, a coffee bar, or your workplace – and you will not only find yourself being preached at politically, but policed for your adherence to 'correct' opinions. Those who disagree are subject to so-called 'cancel culture' and risk being ostracised, re-educated, publicly hounded and humiliated by social media mobs, or simply fired – as happened to Sir Roger Scruton at the hands of the Conservative party. Mr Cobley put it well in his analysis of the 'system of diversity':

One of the system's strengths is the way it makes its opposition appear outside the sphere of acceptable life. These opponents appear as noises from off-stage: as rebels, not just against all that is good but against reality and progress. Even with a Conservative government and the Brexit vote, progressives remain in charge of the stage, dominating what appears in our public space and how it appears.

That system, as we will see in the next chapter, is profoundly flawed, leading to practical failure and widespread unpopularity. It is also increasingly inescapable. 🖋

CHAPTER EIGHT

Failing Upwards

Generally the better educated are more prone to *ir*rational political opinions and political hysteria than the worse educated far from power. Why? In the field of political opinion they are *more* driven by fashion, a gang mentality, and the desire to pose about moral and political questions all of which exacerbate cognitive biases, encourage groupthink, and reduce accuracy.

Dominic Cummings,
'On the referendum #21', 9 January 2017

1. Identify a respected institution.
2. kill it.
3. gut it.
4. wear its carcass as a skin suit, while demanding respect.
#lefties

David Burge (@iowahawk), Twitter, 10 November 2015

When Michael Gove said in June 2016, just before the Brexit referendum, that 'We've had enough of experts', he was pilloried by the expert class. With characteristic self-involvement, they made his jibe one of the most controversial statements of the entire campaign. He had, of course, hit a nerve. The long decade that stretched from the 2008 financial crisis to Boris Johnson's general election victory in December 2019 has been a decade of disillusion. Year by year, the public has come to see that the political and media class that had assumed so much power and made so many grand promises was, in fact, incompetent.

Gordon Brown, New Labour's chancellor of the Exchequer, announced in 1999 that his party had set out to 'end damaging economic instability – to tackle the Tory boom and bust' and that it had succeeded. His self-confidence was toxic. Thanks to

New Labour, Britain walked into the economic storm of 2008 dangerously exposed. In 2010, the outgoing chief secretary to the Treasury, Liam Byrne, left a note for the incoming coalition government: 'I'm afraid there's no money left.' We've been paying ever since. Post-crisis efforts to avoid systemic financial collapse and to restore the public finances have left us with a legacy of bailouts, quantitative easing, austerity and – not least – a resurgent socialism among the young.

Over the last three years, meanwhile, the British public has watched the astonishing spectacle of the political class ripping through protocol and employing every trick of influence in an effort to scupper Brexit and prevent Britain leaving the EU – even as it was plain for all to see that the elite's apocalyptic predictions for the aftermath of a vote to leave were nonsense. As John Gray wrote in the *New Statesman* in January: 'The single most important lesson of the previous three and more years is the abject incompetence of Britain's centrist political class.'

In 2017, Dominic Cummings suggested that the public's view that 'the experts' had failed was a major factor in the Leave vote:

All those amazed at why so little attention was paid to 'the experts' did not, and still do not, appreciate that those 'experts' are seen by most people of all political views as having botched financial regulation, made a load of rubbish predictions, then forced everybody else outside London to pay for the mess while they got richer and dodged responsibility. *They are right. This is exactly what happened.*

This is not an isolated phenomenon. Something very similar has happened in America, where a technocratic ruling class failed to address – or even notice – problems in the wider country, beyond their centres of power; this provided an opportunity for Donald Trump to gain the presidency, as an outsider promising reform. Law professor and Instapundit blogger Glenn Reynolds wrote an article in 2017 for *USA Today* entitled 'Trump and the Crisis of Meritocracy', describing the fallout:

In the United States, the result has been Trump. In Britain, the result was Brexit. In both cases, the allegedly elite – who are supposed to be cool, considered, and above the vulgar passions of the masses – went more or less crazy. From conspiracy theories (it was the Russians!) to bizarre escape fantasies (A Brexit vote redo! A military coup to oust Trump!) the cognitive elite suddenly didn't seem especially elite, or for that matter particularly cognitive.

What went wrong? An important part of the answer is managerialism, the technocratic philosophy of the political class. As an approach, managerialism works well in a highly predictable world. The so-called 'Great Moderation' of economic volatility of the 1990s and 2000s may have given today's political class the time it needed to establish itself – and to become dangerously over-confident. But when the unexpected happens, as it always does, an approach that relies on management of the future through top-down planning is at a loss.

The problem is compounded by managerialism's tendency to undermine itself. It talks up the brilliance of those at the top of the system and sneers at the uneducated. It commits to grand modernist projects to remake institutions and society that seduce the public, and then leave that public resentful when they inevitably fail. It also drives out professionalism, with its interest in the formation of individual character, replacing it with self-interest managed with incentives. Yuval Levin's recent book *A Time to Build* argues that America's institutions have increasingly become platforms on which elite egos enlarge themselves, while neglecting the inner discipline that true leadership demands. As Mr Levin wrote in the *New York Times* in January 2020, 'We lose faith in an institution when we no longer believe that it plays this ethical or formative role of teaching the people within it to be trustworthy.'

Instead, the system produces individuals who are plausible and ambitious, but who live in a world of ideas divorced from any feedback as to their truth. They tend to lack both practical experience of real life and what the author Nassim Taleb calls 'skin in the game' – bearing little risk if their work produces bad outcomes. This does not stop them from enthusiastically trying to control other people's lives. Mr Taleb has a name for this product of managerial culture: the IYI. It stands for 'intellectual yet idiot' – people who are smart on paper, but stupid in practice. As he points out, those who have been living under the thumb of IYIs are now fighting back:

> What we have been seeing worldwide, from India to the UK to the US, is the rebellion against the inner circle of no-skin-in-the-game policymaking 'clerks' and journalists-insiders, that class of paternalistic semi-intellectual experts with some Ivy league, Oxford-Cambridge, or similar label-driven education who are telling the rest of us 1) what to do, 2) what to eat, 3) how to speak, 4) how to think… and 5) who to vote for.

Managerialism not only staffs institutions with IYIs, it also treats the institutions themselves as abstract and inter-changeable units, hollowing out their particular purpose. A patchwork of distinctive and local professional cultures, each emergent from the goals of its individual institution, is replaced by a network of interchangeable workplaces for a single managerial class, standard-bearers of a shared managerial culture. This borderless network has no immunity to the spread of bad ideas. A managerial fad will infect the entire institutional network, if the fad suits the ambition of the managerial class. Such fads are often destructive.

That is because the managerial elite's structure actively selects for bad ideas. To catch on, a fad needs to be counter-intuitive. If it was widely accepted or obvious, there would be no need to promote it and no status to be gained by doing so. However, ideas that violate common sense are rarely correct. If there is no mechanism to weed out the ideas that don't work in practice, bad ideas will dominate. And as we have seen, the managerial class is notorious for lacking 'skin in the game'. Without that reality check to catch counter-intuitive ideas that don't work, managerialism becomes a breeding ground for the opposite of common sense.

We encountered earlier Thomas Sowell's observation that university humanities and sociology departments provide havens where incorrect ideas can endure. Both coaches for college athletics and faculty members who study the hard sciences must constantly test their ideas against reality. Academics working in the softer subjects, however, lack that rigour and are less likely to spot or correct their errors. This is generally true in every institutional environment, where limited information means that reliable predictions cannot be made and where there are no feedback mechanisms for learning. For example, the prime minister's right-hand man, Mr Cummings, has observed this effect in the political arena:

> Neither condition [information for reliable prediction-making and improvement via feedback] applies generally to politics or the political media. In the most rigorous studies done, it has been shown that in general political experts are little better than the proverbial dart throwing chimp and that those most confident in their big picture views and most often on TV – people like Robert Peston, Jon Snow, and Evan Davis – are the least accurate political 'experts'.

This applies even more generally across the political class and the quangocracy. It is true that managerialism relies on targets; but its targets frequently become detached from their intended purpose. Symbolic box-ticking allows managers to appear effective, while insulating them from actual outcomes. They are free to pursue the opposite of common sense with impunity.

Over time, this all helps the steady shift of the managerial class towards leftism. But the corollary is just as important: to the extent that an institution becomes more concerned with promoting a left-wing agenda over time, it will also become less concerned with its original purpose. The Church of England ends up making plans to switch off all its heaters to save the planet, instead of focusing on saving souls. The Arts Council stops using the word 'artist' or defending great art. The Baftas exclude films from consideration on political grounds. In the United States,

Professor John M. Ellis makes the case that the politicisation of the university system through affirmative action introduced a strand of increasingly radical leftism which hurt those whom the system was trying to help:

> And so, while the original intent of [racial] preferences was to provide an education for upward mobility, what preferences actually did was, by promoting campus political radicalism, to block access to that kind of education.

When institutions give up on their core goals, abandon common sense for intellectual fads and fail to form trustworthy individuals, those at the top don't notice: instead, they get philanthropic awards and supportive coverage from their peers. But those who rely on the institutions do notice. That is especially true of those on the geographical periphery of power. Near the centre, narratives of success and technocratic competence hold sway, thanks to the concentration of the ruling class. Out of their sight and mind, such control cannot be maintained. Again, managerialism undermines itself: by assuming that it should ignore most people for the greater good, and by building an enlightened, centralised elite, it walls itself off from evidence of its own failure. America's coastal cities could not see the problems in 'flyover country' that drove the voters there to back Mr Trump. Britain's Westminster bubble could not see the Brexit vote brewing outside the capital. Jeremy Corbyn's Labour party was relying on its Red Wall holding across the Midlands and the North. From Islington, it could not see the cracks forming.

All of this has been made much worse for elites by the information revolution. In 2014, a former CIA analyst called Martin Gurri self-published *The Revolt of the Public and the Crisis of Authority in the New Millennium*, since when Mr Gurri's compelling thesis has been widely praised. His book is credited with foreseeing the rise of Mr Trump to the presidency and explaining the worldwide efflorescence of populist revolt in recent years. He sees the extraordinary democratisation in access to information brought by the internet as a tidal wave that destroys elite authority. Ordinary people now have access to countless sources and archives, and the means to share the information freely. The gleaming modernist façade of managerial efficiency is torn away, and behind the curtain are flawed, corrupt human beings looking out for themselves. The result is disillusion – and distrust. Mr Gurri laid out the results in an essay for *Smith* magazine:

> democratic governments everywhere are haemorrhaging authority and legitimacy at a frightful rate. The public feels disenfranchised by the governing class. Elites believe barbarians have conquered the precincts of power. The two sides know it wasn't always like this, and are gripped by a vertiginous sense of decline and fall – of the decadence of the moment. The numbers support this subjective notion. In the days of John F. Kennedy and Harold Macmillan, between 70 and 80% of the public regularly said they trusted the government. Today trust has fallen to between 20 and 30%.

Those disruptive technological tools also allow the crowd to shout back and self-organise to protest as never before. Mr Gurri sees the Leave referendum campaign as a prime example:

> Cummings, with his 'hack the medium, hack the message' mantra, was among the few responsible parties during the campaign who understood this altered landscape. He invested 98% of Leave's advertising budget in social media, churning out nearly a billion digital ads. While Cameron obsessed over the news cycle, Leave advocates on the web outnumbered and out-energized their opponents.

Mr Cummings, of course, repeated that success in the 2019 general election. In politics, at least, the elite's failings have at last been punished, with the help of the new information environment.

But despite Mr Gurri's revolt of the internet-enabled public and despite the public failings of the political class, outside government the old order remains in place. It is this unnerving stability – a sense that a seismic election victory still hasn't really changed the deeper structures of cultural power – that troubled so many thoughtful Conservatives after Mr Johnson's win.

Václav Havel would have understood what is going on in Britain today. The late Czech statesman – a former dissident against his country's communist government who became president during the Velvet Revolution of 1989 – was intimately acquainted with a government that held onto power despite its own bankruptcy. In 1978, he wrote *The Power of the Powerless*, a classic expression of life in a regime that didn't work, but that required everyone to keep their mouths shut. It contains a famous passage about a greengrocer who puts up a sign supplied by the communist party, declaring 'Workers of the world, unite!' What, Mr Havel asks, does the sign really mean?

> Verbally, it might be expressed this way: 'I, the greengrocer XY, live here and I know what I must do. I behave in the manner expected of me. I can be depended upon and am beyond reproach. I am obedient and therefore I have the right to be left in peace.' This message, of course, has an addressee: it is directed above, to the greengrocer's superior, and at the same time it is a shield that protects the greengrocer from potential informers.

Mr Havel argued that a 'post-totalitarian' system that did not rely simply on direct force and intimidation to impose its will could, nonetheless, exert an unbreakable control over its citizens through this kind of requirement for ideological correctness. The greengrocer does not believe the sign, but fear of the consequences keeps him obedient. Further, the 'ideological excuse' – that the sign is superficially in favour of a higher cause – allows the greengrocer to lie to himself that his behaviour is not cowardice and a breach of conscience. If it said, 'I am afraid and therefore unquestioningly obedient', he would not be able to ignore the truth:

This explains why ideology plays such an important role in the post-totalitarian system: that complex machinery of units, hierarchies, transmission belts, and indirect instruments of manipulation which ensure in countless ways the integrity of the regime, leaving nothing to chance, would be quite simply unthinkable without ideology acting as its all-embracing excuse and as the excuse for each of its parts.

Today's politically correct shibboleths serve the same function. They are a network of control masked behind noble sentiments. And they are just as hard to escape.

The economist Timur Kuran has offered a general theory that explains this kind of ideological logjam through a 'dual preference' model. This builds on the observation that people have two kinds of preferences: those that they hold in private and those that they express in public. Our publicly expressed preferences may disguise our private preferences for social reasons. Mr Kuran calls this process 'preference falsification'. The sign in the greengrocer's shop expresses a public opinion; but because of the social pressures at work, it is impossible to tell if it reflects the grocer's private opinion.

Where public opinion is forced in one direction, as in Czechoslovakia under communism, it becomes impossible to know what anyone really thinks. Everyone is lying to everyone else – and using ideology to excuse their behaviour. In that hall of mirrors, private opposition to the regime can be widespread, but nonetheless ineffective. No one knows how many others would prefer more freedom, and no one wants to acknowledge their own complicity in supporting the status quo. Communism endures, even if there is a private-opinion majority for its overthrow. The Czech regime continued for 20 years after Mr Havel's landmark essay.

Nor is preference falsification unique to undemocratic societies. Mr Kuran also gives an American example: the durability of racial affirmative action. This has persisted for decades, despite clear evidence from polling that there is a substantial private preference for equal treatment, rather than a race-based policy of special treatment. An unpopular policy remains in force because it is socially impossible to express that disagreement in public. In Britain, too, the political and media class exerts huge pressure for cultural conformity. The Brexit referendum and 2019 general election results were possible because they were private ballots. The 'shy Tory' or 'shy Brexiteer' effect, where voters won't even admit to pollsters who they will vote for, is proof that Conservative preferences are crowded out of public discourse.

Proof of this in the arts came from an anonymous poll conducted in 2020 by *Arts Professional*. An astonishing 80 per cent of respondents agreed that any individuals working in the arts who 'share controversial opinions risk being professionally ostracised'. 'Controversial' opinions included right-wing politics and views that challenged the industry consensus on gender and sexuality, as well as on public subsidies. In the words of one submission: '[The arts] are now dominated by a monolithic, politically correct class (mostly of privileged white middle-class people) who impose their intolerant views.'

Suppression of different opinions is the real danger when institutions begin to serve a political cause. People often imagine that the risk of being fed a cultural diet of leftist propaganda is indoctrination. The reality is more subtle and far harder to resist. One-sided public propaganda from authoritative sources – whether schools, the BBC or even popular celebrities – establishes 'correct' public opinion as common knowledge. It ensures that you know what you are expected to say. Like Havel's greengrocer, you do not need to be privately persuaded that these views are correct in order to feel trapped into conformity. A one-sided culture keeps itself in power not by winning every heart and mind – it endures because those who oppose it privately dare not risk breaking the public consensus.

However, such stability is brittle. Any regime that relies on suppressing public expression is, as a result, also in the dark about the strength of private preferences. It has no idea if opposition is gathering beneath the surface. If it does, Mr Kuran's model shows that relatively small shifts in publicly expressed opinion can trigger a runaway effect: a sudden, unstoppable shift in public opinion, which Mr Kuran terms a 'preference cascade'. This explains the sudden, unpredicted collapse of Eastern Europe's communist regimes in 1989.

A preference cascade is a true overnight revolution in public culture. When Mr Havel became president, he was joined by several other ex-dissidents. One, Jiří Dienstbier, had been working as a coal stoker before the revolution. So sudden was Mr Dienstbier's elevation that the day he was appointed Czechoslovakia's foreign secretary he also had to dash back to work and finish stoking his assigned boiler.

As if a switch has been flipped, a preference cascade reverses the status of publicly held opinions. The public rapidly settles into a fresh equilibrium, and preference falsification then ensures that even previous hardliners express public preferences in line with the new reality. After communism fell in 1989, it was hard to find anyone who professed to having been in favour of the old regimes.

The problem with preference cascades is that they are infrequent and unpredictable. No one saw 1989 coming, including the dissidents who were working for the overthrow of communism. Mr Havel was one of the most perceptive critics: he saw that a bloodless and sudden overthrow was possible. Nevertheless, even he was caught off guard when it happened. In October 1988, only a year before Mr Havel became president, a group of dissidents published a manifesto entitled 'Demokracii pro všechny' ('Democracy for All'). Mr Havel wrote: 'Perhaps it will remain for the time being merely the seed of something that will bear fruit in the dim and distant future. It is equally possible that the entire "matter" will be stamped on hard.'

In the absence of a preference cascade, a system built on preference falsification – whether a communist government or a politically correct democratic elite – can be remarkably durable. By establishing which political choices are in fashion, and by cracking down on criticism, it strengthens not just public, but even private support. By hiding the extent of disagreement, it obscures both the need for reform and its possibility. Mr Kuran's analysis shows that public opinion can remain frozen even in the face of a system's clear failure: 'When new conditions make a once-popular decision appear to have been a mistake, or when a once-functional structure becomes patently dysfunctional, public opinion will not necessarily adjust.' In 1984, a survey of Polish workers found that only 16 per cent were satisfied with their socialist government. Yet most could not escape the idea drummed into them that socialism was the only just political order. When asked 'Do you think the world should develop toward some other form of socialism?' only 28 per cent disagreed. Three in five favoured 'social ownership of the means of production'.

Britain's post-Blairite political class – the final product of the left's long march into our institutions – has failed. It has been rejected decisively at the ballot box. And yet throughout our culture, the leftist Blob remains, its unpopular errors sustained by managerial blindness and preference falsification. Without the (unpredictable) arrival of a cascade to overturn our dysfunctional elite, this situation could continue indefinitely. But there are other ways to fight back. ⌐

CHAPTER NINE

The Art of Cultural Resistance

I have been doing better. But somehow the things drift back again: the stubborn beast-flesh grows day by day back again. But I mean to do better things still. I mean to conquer that. This puma—

H.G. Wells, *The Island of Doctor Moreau*, 1896

The conceptual challenge posed to a particular cosmology may render it less and less credible and eventually precipitate a crisis in thought. But this will not necessarily lead to a new cosmology. Other conditions must exist for that to happen, most particularly the formulation of an acceptable new paradigm.

Paul Gottfried, *After Liberalism: Mass Democracy in the Managerial State*, 2001

In *The Wizard of Oz*, once Dorothy discovers the truth about Oz the Great and Powerful, his authority collapses like a pricked balloon. We, however, do not live in that story. To see behind the curtain is not enough to release us from the humbug wizardry of our political class. Yet, by seeing our predicament square on, we can start to think clearly about how to break the deadlock. Many counter-offensives are proposed or are already being pursued. Given the success of the left's long march through our institutions, and the curious hybrid of liberal-left managerialism that won the day, which strategies best suit the task of cultural resistance?

The simplest and most optimistic course is patience. If current trends are unsustainable, then they can be left to collapse of their own accord, or be corrected by market forces. The slogan 'get woke, go broke' points to the commercial failure of some attempts to put identity politics before audience satisfaction. There is truth to this: the all-female reboot in 2016 of *Ghostbusters* was a notable flop. However, within the narrative of the left's culture warriors, such failures only prove the depth of popular prejudice and deepen their commitment to mass re-education. In any case, many key British institutions – the BBC, state schools, the quangocracy – are not shaped by commercial pressures. And even those that are operate within an environment where their elite peers and institutional dynamics push them toward the left, while their customers' protests are limited by preference falsification.

There is no guarantee that the current situation will resolve itself. As Douglas Murray says in *The Madness of Crowds*, 'People looking for this movement to wind down because of its inherent contradictions will be waiting a long time.' When the policing of language for political correctness first emerged in the Nineties, it was easy to see it as a passing fad. Back then, the control now being exerted over speech – with the police actually turning up at people's workplaces because they have expressed a (non-criminal) opinion of their own – would have seemed unimaginable. The movement has yet to show any sign that it will be brought down by its own contradictions or its illiberal tendencies; and while it lasts, the costs to those who disagree could very well get higher. Similarly, the repeated, public failures of our elite have not dethroned them from their cultural eyries.

Since patience will not work, another strategy which avoids head-on conflict is self-imposed exile. The American author and blogger Rod Dreher calls this the Benedict Option. He argues that culturally conservative Christians should accept that they cannot win the culture war, that they are doomed to increasing attacks from the elite, and that they should move to the periphery and work to build communities centred on their values. Fans of Ayn Rand will be familiar with the related idea of 'going Galt' – dropping out of a statist society to starve it of your productive contributions. A less ideological version might be called the *Firefly* Option, after the science fiction television show in which a group of rebels, having lost the war against an autocratic empire, scratch out a semi-criminal living on its periphery.

Mr Dreher makes a serious case for conscious withdrawal from the culture. He points to the dilemma of the greengrocer in Václav Havel's *Power of the Powerless* and asks how to find a durable way of life that escapes the left-liberal empire's requirement for public lying. When you do not expect the culture to shift, and fear it will only get worse, isolating yourself from the worst excesses is an understandable response. There is no dishonour in taking such a route.

However, the reach of the social engineers is already long, and it is not clear that it can be escaped, even at the periphery. Should you 'go Firefly' and manage to avoid wealth taxes, woke police, politically correct workplaces and ideologically slanted schools, rule by the managerial class also produces failures that you cannot insulate yourself against – like the financial crisis and its aftermath.

Such a choice also means giving up all opportunity for changing the culture. Those who argue for it often fudge this point. By calling it the Benedict Option, Mr Dreher points to the foundation of the monastic tradition that was a vital thread in the survival and renaissance of Western civilisation. Ms Rand's drop-outs step back from society to bring down the system.

It doesn't work like that. The distinguished academic James Davison Hunter, who brought the term 'culture war' to popular prominence with his 1991 book *Culture Wars: The Struggle to Define America*, has shown through historical analysis that cultures are changed by networks close to the centre of elite power. Monasteries were physically isolated, but deeply connected to power, patronage and elite intellectual life. The great scholar-monk Alcuin of York was able to lead the Carolingian renaissance because of his place at the court of Charlemagne. Ms Rand imagined characters who changed the world by leaving it; but her real influence came through her place in the intellectual networks of twentieth-century America.

This helps explain the contemporary importance of universities in the cultural battle. Fears over student indoctrination get more attention, but the primary significance of academia is as a meeting point where elite power, top minds and new ideas collide. Universities provide a setting within which small networks of very clever people – like the Frankfurt School – can come together and develop new ideas in a sustained fashion over many years. The university setting gives those ideas legitimacy and spreads them through its networks of students, staff and alumni.

Mr Davison Hunter likes to quote his mentor, Peter Berger, a great scholar of religious sociology, who put it this way: 'Ideas don't succeed in history because of their inherent truthfulness but rather because of their connection to very powerful institutions and interests.' Mr Davison Hunter himself proposes a Christian cultural strategy of 'faithful presence', which does not expect influence, but nonetheless commits itself to remaining visible in cultural production and social life at the highest level.

'Faithful presence' comes closer to the stance of dissidents under communism. These individuals, like Mr Havel, neither tried to wait out their oppression nor tried to avoid it. Instead, they kept speaking up and arguing against the mainstream, even at considerable cost to themselves.

Today, while the stakes are less extreme, taking a stand can still mean personal and professional ostracism, vile abuse and even death threats. There are a number of individuals willing to face that risk: from the actor Laurence Fox and the comedian Andrew Doyle (creator of Titania McGrath) to James Lindsay and Helen Pluckrose, who questioned the intellectual rigour of certain fashionable types of 'cultural studies' by writing absurd fake papers that were accepted by academic journals.

Their rebellion is valuable. It provides models for resistance and dissent, and offers a public reminder that other views exist and can be expressed. In Martin Gurri's terms, their mockery and irreverence also serve to chip away at the authority of corrupt institutions. However, the public vitriol directed at those who step out of line also keeps the number of rebels small. As a result, such dissent is not enough in itself to change the culture. According to Timur Kuran, men like Mr Havel consider honest self-expression more important than anything else. This allows them to stand up, at the cost of personal ruin and isolation, even while they know their protest will not make a difference. Such individuals are admirable, and they are rare.

However, the ability of individual online influencers, including those with heterodox opinions, to build audiences in the millions through online platforms does provide a new and promising avenue for cultural influence. In a fascinating recent example from America, the *New York Times* editorial board announced that, instead of picking one candidate, it was endorsing the two female candidates in the race for the Democratic presidential nomination: Amy Klobuchar and Elizabeth Warren. This had little effect on public opinion, despite the *Times'* traditional status as America's newspaper of record. Far more significant for public opinion was the declaration of support for Bernie Sanders by comedian and podcaster Joe Rogan. Mr Rogan has 5.7 million followers on Twitter alone.

Celebrities have an almost magical ability to transfer their authority to whatever they endorse. They need have no prior expertise or special connection to whatever they are endorsing. The effect relies on the size of their fanbase and the automatic transfer of positive emotional associations by fans from a celebrity to anything he or she endorses. This is why great athletes are sought after to promote luxury watches, and why music and film stars are encouraged by activists to make political endorsements.

The conventional celebrity worlds have long been dominated by the left. Think of the pro-Corbyn statements of Stormzy, or the rapper Dave, who denounced Mr Johnson as a racist on stage at the 2020 Brit awards. When the singer Taylor Swift attempted to remain apolitical, she was subjected to a campaign of pressure, until she gave in and produced the pro-LGBT 'You Need to Calm Down'. But the world of online celebrity is still evolving, and it provides new opportunities for ideas outside the liberal-left bubble to benefit from the endorsement effect. Because this all seems so shallow, it may be hard to take seriously; but the effect is real, and its full potential remains to be realised.

This effect becomes even more powerful when, instead of relying on a single, short-lived celebrity brand, it is combined with the creation of a new and enduring institution. We saw how the success of the Fabians was connected with their early gift for establishing new bodies to develop and spread their views. Today, many well-established institutions, especially in the media, are in crisis, with their business models and authority challenged by the internet. New entrants have a rare opportunity to enter the market, build online celebrity and share points of view that would otherwise not be heard, reaching large audiences. Online magazines like *Quillette*, and YouTube chat shows like the New Culture Forum's *So What You're Saying Is* and *CounterCulture* are examples of how this can work. In America, the stars of the *Daily Wire*, like Andrew Klavan, and Dave Rubin of the *Rubin Report* reach huge audiences, while challenging the mainstream, liberal-left narrative.

Even without the celebrity effect, there are huge opportunities to form new countercultural institutions. The lack of gatekeepers online and the existence of large groups unhappy with the cultural centre make it possible to build significant audiences for countercultural messages. The opportunities include not just commentary, but original work in the creative arts – something that Mr Klavan of the *Daily Wire* both champions and practises, with his *Another Kingdom* fiction podcast. As we saw in chapter 8, expression in the mainstream art world is tightly constrained. But new institutions can let new voices be heard.

Another vital role for new institutions is defending the rights of dissenters, through public support and legal action. Two examples from the UK are Toby Young's Free Speech Union, designed to protect those who are attacked for expressing their views, and Fair Cop, formed by Harry Miller, who took the police to court for their attempts to suppress his freedom of speech.

A more academic model is the University of Buckingham's new Vinson Centre for Economics and Entrepreneurship, a space where the ideas at the heart of the Thatcher revolution can be studied by a new generation of academics. In America, the Claremont Institute is remarkably productive and effective. It publishes a highbrow intellectual journal, *The Claremont Review of Books*, and engages in serious and original analysis of America's political challenges. It sponsors fellowships, in which talented young individuals are introduced to the Claremont perspective on the principles of the American founding, before they go on to careers at the heart of the Washington establishment. And it recently created an online media platform called *The American Mind*, which publishes carefully argued, often provocative views on the ideas behind political life.

New institutions are vital, and are only likely to grow in importance as their traditional rivals struggle in the face of technological and economic disruption. Yet cultural change, as Mr Davison Hunter observes, happens near the centre of elite power. New institutions may grow into that kind of authority, but for now they are most effective when they develop their own influential superpowers through online celebrity, or when they help shape the agenda of the mainstream. The Claremont fellowships are a good example of how to do the latter. Closer to home, consider how the Brexit party was not effective as an electoral force in the 2019 general election, but was nonetheless influential on the Conservatives, both as a source of policy ideas and as a means of restricting Mr Johnson's room for manoeuvre on Brexit. Equally, President Trump uses new media, especially Twitter, to promote his messages, but the real power of this is his ability to provoke the mainstream media into covering his tweets, giving him enormous amounts of unpaid publicity.

Failure to understand this last point risks becoming trapped in a new media bubble – as happened, for example, to Labour in the recent general election. It was thrilled by the fact that it outperformed the Conservatives on Twitter: Corbyn received 2.4 million retweets, compared to 372,000 for the Conservatives; and Labour also had three times as many video views. However, the crucial demographics in the election did not get their news from social media, and Labour had not considered the need to project that influence out into the mainstream.

The most successful new institutions for lasting cultural change exploit the latest technology, but they also combine with elite connections, access to significant funding, top minds and the development of bold new ideas. Think tanks have always appreciated the power of this combination. Both the Fabian Society and the free marketeers behind the Thatcher revolution had intellectuals of the highest calibre, with their public authority guaranteed by Nobel Prizes (literature for George Bernard Shaw and economics prizes for Friedrich Hayek and

Milton Friedman). Both groups developed sophisticated and original ideas that spread over several decades through elite networks until they changed British culture in permanent ways.

Likewise, the Frankfurt School's influence relied on brilliant minds, intellectual innovation and access to the elite intellectual networks of post-war America. It also relied on exceptionally generous patronage. According to Mr Davison Hunter's research, Felix Weil's father, Hermann, not only financed the original building and equipment and gave the IfS an endowment of 3.5 million marks, but he then also provided a further annual grant of 120,000 marks. The faculty had 10 permanent academic staff.

For a more recent example, consider the most successful culture-shaping institution in America, the Federalist Society. It was founded as a student organisation in 1982 – note the university setting – and promoted a literal legal reading of the US constitution based on its original meaning. The society provided an institutional home for a clear, intellectually well-argued alternative to the progressive 'living constitution' model then dominant in American law schools. New generations of the most promising legal professionals were exposed to its influence. Nearly four decades later, it boasts four justices of the US Supreme Court as its members, including both of President Trump's appointees.

The idea of Brexit itself followed a long, slow course. It required decades of commitment and a few highly placed figures willing to develop the case and argue for it, even when they were swimming against the intellectual tide. Transformational ideas can end up taking control, but this requires the development of a credible alternative, guaranteed by established elite markers of excellence and spread through elite intellectual networks over many years.

Changing the culture through the institutions is possible, but the only route that evidently works is at the highest level. It is expensive, demanding, uncertain and, above all, frustratingly slow. Fabius, the military commander whose gradualist strategy inspired the Fabians, was always a controversial figure in Rome. He was only allowed to resume his strategy after a more direct attempt to engage the enemy ended in a crushing defeat at Cannae.

One should be careful about taking the Marxist radicals – who were wrong about almost everything – at face value. They were certainly wrong to imagine that human nature was infinitely malleable in the face of different economic and cultural conditions. In 1969, Herbert Marcuse suggested in his *Essay on Liberation* that human nature itself would have to change, in order for the revolution to succeed:

> the radical change which is to transform the existing society into a free society must reach into a dimension of the human existence hardly considered in Marxian theory – the *biological* dimension in which the vital, imperative needs and satisfactions of man assert themselves. Inasmuch as these needs and satisfactions reproduce a life in servitude, liberation presupposes changes in this biological dimension, that is to say, different instinctual needs, different reactions of the body as well as the mind.

The resilience of human nature continues to provide a bulwark against such plans to utterly remake our society. But the radicals did better when they moved away from the original dream of remaking the proletariat into a radical force and stumbled upon the credulity, malleability and creative energy to be found within the intellectual class. Here, ideas could take root without the need to prove their truth, and would spread through institutional networks, gaining the power to influence an entire society from above.

Today, that insight holds true. Those who want to escape such cultural control cannot simply wait patiently for the system to collapse. A brave few will stand up and express dissent, but they must accept their punishment and cannot expect to change the world. Some will do their best to distance themselves from the regime's power, but they will also distance themselves from any ability to change its nature.

The best hope for cultural warfare today is to create new institutions and seize fresh opportunities for influence, such as online celebrity. But such attempts need to be designed with an understanding of the necessary conditions for cultural influence. A rejection of the established order is not enough. It takes a generation and requires sophisticated new ideas, shared at the centre through high-status institutions. In the words of Mr Davison Hunter, 'culture is as much infrastructure as it is ideas'.

A slow revolution from the left has seized Britain's elite culture. But there is a glimmer of hope: Brexit has now taken back political control. The question for Mr Johnson is whether he has the necessary ambition and dedication to use politics to take back the culture.

CHAPTER TEN

Downstream of Politics

… the ultimate purpose of this Government is not economic but moral. You were elected to give back to individuals a greater degree of responsibility for the conduct of their own lives.

Oliver Letwin, in a private memo to Mrs Thatcher, 1986

The central conservative truth is that it is culture, not politics, that determines the success of a society. The central liberal truth is that politics can change a culture and save it from itself.

Daniel Patrick Moynihan, Family and Nation: The Godkin Lectures, 1986

The culture war for Britain's institutions has been lost – not to the communists and socialists who once dreamed of a Gramscian march to hegemony, but to the political class. Left-liberal heirs of Blair, but long past mere party allegiance, this self-serving, interconnected Blob dominates our centralised elite. Their status insulates them from the consequences of their failures, while the harm falls, unheard, on those living on the periphery. As managerialists, they prefer counterintuitive proposals to common sense, targets over real effects, and power above everything else. They have, therefore, embraced the promotion of diversity and inclusion and radical environmentalism, instead of focusing on the original goals of their institutions. While Margaret Thatcher's counter-revolution successfully inoculated the political class against the economics of the hard left, it had no immunity against cultural ideas from the same stable. Radical, divisive theories of patriarchal and racial oppression and of the need to overturn our economic system for the sake of the planet had been refined over decades in academic networks. Now they have gained cultural purchase, by enchanting a class so proud of its own neutral rationality that it cannot see the danger.

Recapturing the cultural heights with fresh ideas will take decades. Yet the left's takeover has, ironically, driven it further from political power. A Conservative government is in Downing Street with a secure majority. Barring a huge reversal in the polls, Boris Johnson's party could hold power for a decade or more. And Mr Johnson's victory would have been impossible without the long march through the institutions. The fight against Brexit revealed to the public the unified nature of Britain's political class, its cross-party contempt for democracy, its incompetence and its distance from the values of many voters.

As cultural exiles, the Conservatives had a unique opportunity to present themselves as the party for those who opposed the elite consensus. By expelling or driving out those MPs whose first loyalty was to the political class, and by placing a Brexiteer at the helm, the Conservative party was adapted for political success by cultural means. And as we have already seen, the private nature of elections protects voting from the mechanism of preference falsification that gives the left so much of its cultural power. On 13 December, the results spoke for themselves.

The political environment is also turning more generally against the modern left. A number of observers, notably Dr Stephen Davies, have pointed out that we are in the middle of a global realignment in politics. The issues of primary concern are turning from economics to identity, with the broad elite consensus for globalisation and market solutions under attack.

In this new landscape, parties of the right across the world have shown themselves more nimble, able to adjust their economic policies somewhat leftward, while embracing the patriotic values for which they have retained a strong affinity. It has proven far harder, thanks to the left's institutional dominance, for parties of the left to shift rightward on these cultural topics. Instead, the cultural theories of the academic and intellectual left have been devoted to problematising ordinary common sense. Jeremy Corbyn's history of support for

Britain's enemies made him an unconvincing patriot, even to longstanding Labour voters. Similarly, the current candidates for the Labour leadership feel compelled to express support for 'woke' causes which engage the activist centre in London, but harm their chances with voters on the cultural periphery.

Seeking to dominate culture, the left was drawn to the elite intellectual networks through which such power is exerted. Ironically, the result has been that a movement created to liberate the lower orders now faces a class revolt from below, with the uneducated mass using the ballot box to reject an educated class won over to the totalitarian nonsense of the cultural left.

Yet at the same time, the right's alliance with those on the periphery offers no route to recapture the culture, which can only be done from the centre. And while this stalemate continues, the left is radicalising. Today's shift against market economics and the broad loss of authority for existing models have assisted in the resurgence of hard-left policies. Jeremy Corbyn and his followers remain influential in the Labour party in Britain, and the Democratic party in America is increasingly radical, with Bernie Sanders having come within sight of its presidential nomination earlier this year. Open socialists and even communists appear on mainstream media on both sides of the Atlantic, and new media outlets such as *Jacobin* magazine, the *Canary* and *Novara Media* take Marxist ideas seriously and promote them to large audiences.

The long march has, for now, made the left unelectable. But the most radical forms of the left are back on the threshold of political power. One unlucky election could open the door to revolutionary change.

Mr Johnson's position is secure. But the tail risks are too large for him to be comfortable. Possessed of a narrow window of opportunity to seize the post-Brexit initiative, he should take political action to effect cultural change.

While politics is often said to be downstream from culture, the relationship is not so one-way. As we have seen, Mrs Thatcher's economic liberalism was designed not just to create wealth, but to change the very culture of Britain.

101

It is hard to convert the public opinion of an entire country overnight into a transformative cascade, but party loyalties are notoriously shallow. A political party's activists will shift their views between one breath and the next to support a winning leader, even one with a significantly different agenda. In the wake of Theresa May's leadership victory, the Conservative party was instantly full of 'Mayite' enthusiasm for industrial policy and government interventions. But when she lost the party its majority in 2017, her star waned. President Trump, Mrs Thatcher and Mr Corbyn all illustrate the power this offers to change the culture of a party from the top. Not all of the old guard will comply, especially those whose careers are already established and who are less reliant on patronage; but the overall culture does shift.

Once a party has been transformed, it then has considerable power to change the wider culture through political means – through appointments, legislation and public statements. This is especially true at historic turning-points, where a nation is publicly aware of the need for transformative policies – as in 1945, with the creation of the post-war welfare state. And it also helps when such politically led changes build upon a decades-long intellectual effort, such as pre-1945 Fabianism or the free-market movement.

Like Clement Attlee, Mrs Thatcher seized a moment of crisis and led the country in a new direction. As Britain leaves the EU, Mr Johnson has a similar opportunity. However, he will have to think creatively. Two approaches which, at first sight, would appear to offer the obvious answers – either appoint ideological allies to head powerful institutions or set off a 'bonfire of the quangos' – are, on closer examination, unlikely to succeed.

Calls for a rival 'long march through the institutions' from the right are increasingly popular. Andrew Roberts' *Telegraph* article written just after the election (mentioned in chapter 1) is a good example. In it, he called on Mr Johnson to:

> institute a Gramscian counter-march through the institutions, liberating one after the other from the grip of the Left … In five years' time it should be possible to be a

proud Tory in the BBC, a Scottish University, an NHS Trust, the Channel 4 board, or even a major trade union, and not feel that you are carrying The Mark of Cain.

This strategy makes intuitive sense. The left-leaning elite is not part of Mr Johnson's new governing coalition. He does not need their votes and he will never have their support. Given the current monoculture in the quangos, a few well-placed appointments could undoubtedly make a real difference. However, it is not clear that any wholesale shift can be implemented quickly or succeed in the long term.

New Labour had over 10 years in power to implement its strategy of quietly appointing supportive figures to the quangos. The Conservatives should not hope to replicate this in a shorter period or in a more public fashion. The *ConservativeHome* website and the Taxpayers' Alliance have been drawing attention to the lack of Conservatives applying for public appointments since at least 2013, with *ConservativeHome* running its 'Calling Conservatives' feature on new vacancies since 2015, so far with little effect.

In practice, the Conservatives have certain natural disadvantages compared to Labour, making it far harder for them to copy this strategy, even over a decade. Numbers matter. The sway of the educated classes to the liberal-left means that there are far more candidates sympathetic to that point of view. In 2002 (since when the problem has become considerably worse), Chris Woodhead wrote from experience of battling to improve the education establishment:

> ... politicians need professionals to work through the detail and implement their reforms, but most senior figures in education, however cleverly they hide the fact at interview, are enthusiastic supporters of the *status quo* that the Government wants to change.

Ideology is also a factor. The left accepts that state agencies run by experts should be telling all of us how to live and helping us modernise our thought. It follows that many who apply for roles at the top of such agencies are left wing. Those who are concerned about such power – in principle and out of a pragmatic suspicion of its real effects – tend to be Conservative supporters. And to the extent that Conservative individuals do step forward, they are likely to be those most accepting of the system and least interested in reform: political class loyalists.

Then there is the unavoidable bullying and intimidation. The hounding of Sir Roger Scruton and other public appointees like Toby Young was shocking, and in both cases drove two hardened veterans of the culture war from office. It shows how much is still being asked of any Conservative who steps into these hostile environments determined to think differently. The job comes with a target painted on your back.

Even if enough likeminded and courageous individuals could be found to step forward, and their rapid defenestration somehow prevented, the strategy would still be swimming against the tide. These institutions drift to the left for structural reasons, and there is no reason to be confident that even a swathe of 'Conservative' appointees would not, in practice, be captured by the institutional culture and its imperatives. To join the Blob is to be absorbed into the Blob.

Mr Johnson should also resist taking this strategy too far for moral reasons, as well as practical. Beneath the mask of good intentions, any serious attempt at institutional infiltration is a strategy built and sustained by violent intimidation at worst – visible not only in the tactics of the thugs who took over the Polytechnic of North London or who dug up the lawns at Trinity College Cambridge, but also in the Twitter-mobbing of Sir Roger and Mr Young. At its best, any attempt must still rely on misrepresentation and manipulation to be effective. These are destructive tactics, devised by a utopian movement that sought to tear apart a society it despised. They are not a model for those who seek to preserve and rebuild.

The idea of a 'long march from the right' also assumes that there is nothing wrong with an institutional network by which the elite controls the rest of society – only a disagreement over which side should be in charge. Again and again, accepting that short-sighted premise has led Conservatives to create or maintain institutions that fell into the hands of the left, driving today's relentless politicisation of everyday life. As Friedrich Hayek warned in *The Constitution of Liberty*, 'Like the socialist, [the conservative] is less concerned with the problem of how the powers of government should be limited than with that of who wields them.'

A 'long march' from the right is not a realistic solution. Neither is the overnight demolition of the quangocracy. Both Tony Blair and David Cameron promised a bonfire of the quangos: both oversaw their expansion. This approach is as intuitively tempting as the call for a binge of Conservative appointments – and evidently just as unrealistic in practice.

Instead, Mr Johnson must limit the system's worst excesses, while developing a contrasting cultural vision that unites the country.

Making some new, Conservative-minded appointments to public bodies would set the tone for change, but it cannot be the full answer. Plans by Dominic Cummings to reshape Whitehall offer a more promising direction of attack. Mr Cummings is attempting to introduce a new culture, grounded in rigorous testing, where scientific thinking and learning from experimentation replace corrupt managerialism. He credits this approach with his success in the referendum campaign:

> Charlie Munger is one half of the most successful investment partnership in world history. He advises people – hire physicists. It works and the real prize is not the technology but a culture of making decisions in a rational way and systematically avoiding normal ways of fooling yourself as much as possible.

Mr Cummings' approach has the potential to cut through outmoded thinking and bring in outside talent to tackle major national challenges. If he can restructure the civil service, it could be transformative. However, it is a centralising manoeuvre, giving more power to Number 10, which will not always be in Conservative hands. It will also be contested by every means at the political and media establishment's disposal. The character

THE LONG MARCH: How the left won the culture war and what to do about it

assassination and swift resignation of Andrew Sabisky in February sent a clear public message of what can be expected by anyone willing to join Mr Cummings"weirdo squad".

Pending Mr Cummings' reforms, for the bulk of the quangocracy Mr Johnson should follow the strategy that is being taken against the BBC: reject its authority and shrink its scope. It remains to be seen if the licence fee will be scrapped or decriminalised and the BBC drastically pruned back, but this is clearly the right direction. The BBC is an ideal target because of its prominence and because it openly funds an out-of-touch elite through an enforced licence fee that hits the poor hardest. Two additional priorities should be to crack down further on 'sockpuppet' lobby groups that rely on government funds, and to restrict political campaigning by charities.

Another important tactic should be the restoration of the constitutional safeguards bulldozed by Blairite modernisers as the political class came to power. Mr Johnson's apparent commitment to revisit the status of the Supreme Court and overturn Mr Blair's ham-fisted abolition of the role of lord chancellor is a good example of how this could work in practice. Turning away from media leaks and restoring a culture of policy proposals announced in parliament would also be welcome.

Less tangibly, but just as important, Mr Johnson and his government should oppose the ideas of the political class in their language. Mrs Thatcher's speeches and interviews regularly contrasted her belief in the individual to the errors and failures of socialism. President Trump has made a point of publicly resisting political correctness and calling for 'Happy Christmas' to replace 'Happy Holidays'. Today's Conservatives need to draw public attention in plain language to their values, and show how those differ from the values of their elite opponents. Today, the members of the political class are the true reactionaries, babbling jargon as they desperately try to hold onto the privilege they have gained from an old and bankrupt order. The Conservatives should be the party that offers a new and straightforward respect for all. On the one hand, elite managerialism with contempt for ordinary voters; on the other, common sense and citizenship.

This should also include standing against the politically correct tide. The bully pulpit of office is a powerful means to counteract the enforced preference falsification imposed by our institutions. Mr Johnson should draw a clear blue line. On the Conservative side: care for the environment; equality of opportunity; no tolerance of racism or sexism. On the side of the elite: climate emergency as an excuse for overriding democratic safeguards and overthrowing capitalism; speech treated as violence, justifying its stringent control; and the demand for the endless power necessary to impose equality of outcomes.

Finally, Number 10 needs to channel power downwards, into the hands of voters, rather than simply trying to improve the way in which it is wielded. The enduring answer to a corrupt political class is not to try to change its party allegiance. The real alternative is to reject the system that sets meritocratic managerialists over the rest, and return to recognising our equal status as citizens.

Prising power out of the grip of the Blob will not be easy. Mr Johnson needs positive, practical ideas with which he can break the managerial deadlock.

Eight years before Michael Gove said 'we've had enough of experts', Dan Hannan MEP and Douglas Carswell MP co-authored *The Plan*, setting out policies to renew British democracy in just 12 months. *The Plan* contrasts the 'rational constructivism' of the elites to the common-sense British tradition of evolutionary rationalism through common law, subsidiarity and local knowledge. It argues that expert power is unaccountable and undemocratic: '"Putting the experts in charge", means ... excusing government employees from having to answer to the rest of us through our elected tribunes.'

The Plan proposes a rapid course of decentralisation to reinstate our common-sense traditions. Quite apart from the merits of particular proposals, some of which have already been influential, it deserves to be dusted off by Conservative strategists and studied as one of the best intellectual cases against the failed world of expert power. Grounded in an understanding of how culturally alien the managerial state is to our system, Mr Hannan and Mr Carswell saw 12 years ago that the historical responsibility for dispersing power from public-sector monopolies had passed from left to right.

Another essential source for Mr Johnson should be *Mass Flourishing*, by the Nobel Prize-winning economist Edmund Phelps. Debunking the consensus view that capitalism relies on a few elite wealth-creators at the top, Mr Phelps shows that a flourishing and dynamic market economy must be built much lower down:

> … grass-roots dynamism was crucial to the good economy of the past: to material progress, inclusion, and job satisfaction. And restoration of that dynamism will be crucial to the rebirth of the good economy.

Despite his economics background, Mr Phelps understands the importance of culture. He proposes:

> We must reintroduce the main ideas of modern thought, such as individualism and vitalism, into secondary and higher education both to refuel grass-roots dynamism in the economy and to preserve the modern itself.

This has much in common with the revived entrepreneurialism that was one of Mrs Thatcher's most significant cultural achievements. There is still more that can be done. And Mr Phelps' brilliant contribution can help to guide it.

Some changes can be implemented behind the scenes. The regulatory wiring that in certain sectors strangles bottom-up innovation even in private firms – notably both media and education – needs to pruned back hard.

However, to establish a renewed professionalism, focused on achieving primary institutional goals rather than serving managerial fads, change must happen in public view. This will mean taking out layers of management and curtailing top-down initiatives from the centre. Instead, the responsibility – and the savings – should be passed to the front line. This requires trust; but in an age of information abundance, on-the-ground knowledge is still being ignored and shut out by systems designed to work from above. Successful policies of this kind will transform the daily lives of many talented individuals for the better, giving them the necessary freedom to achieve more. It will make the promise of cultural change concrete.

A practical example is the success of teacher-led schools in America, organised as professional partnerships in a similar manner to legal firms. This approach places professionalism at its heart and has, in practice, improved both academic results and teacher retention. In 2014, Gallup surveyed 12 different professions. Teachers were the least likely to agree with the statement 'my opinion seems to matter at work'. Yet an extensive study by Professor Richard Ingersoll of the impact of school leadership found that 'students perform better in schools with the highest levels of instructional and teacher leadership' and 'when teachers are involved in decision-making processes related to school improvement planning and student conduct policies, students learn more'.

This idea was proposed for the UK in the form of Teaching Partnerships by Paul Gray in *A Blue Tomorrow: New Visions for Modern Conservatives*, published in 2001: 'Just as we gave council house tenants discounts and incentives to own their own homes, so too we could give teachers one of the most important aspects of the professions – ownership of their own business.'

Practical initiatives – like teacher-led schools – could allow stressed workers in important sectors to feel the immediate benefits of escaping a managerial culture, while unleashing their talents to improve outcomes. The right political rhetoric can drive home the message that such changes are not piecemeal, but part of a clear direction of travel. The journey is toward a country where we look one another in the eye as political equals, rather than allowing a privileged few to look down on us from the heights of power. By escaping the grip of the political class, we become free to restore the tradition of common-sense citizenship.

Our new government will not succeed in its cultural fight if it tries to step into the shoes of the existing, discredited elite. Instead, it must reject left-liberal managerialism as a broken model. Rather than attempting a counter-march from the right or a radical bonfire of the quangos, its historic task is to be more civilised: restraining and reforming out-of-control institutions, and restoring traditional structures where possible. It must also trust to our native common sense, devolving power away from the centre, while celebrating in public our shared pride in the British tradition. Together, we can then start the long march home after a century of revolution. 🖋

INDEX

2019 General Election, 1–4, 86

Adorno, Theodor, xv, 22–23, 27–28

Blair, Tony, xvii, 51, 55–56, 58–60, 66–67, 99
  and managerialism, 64
  and quangos, 18, 105
Blairism, xvii, xxii, 55, 66, 88, 106
Blob, The, xiv, 19, 64, 88, 99, 104, 107
  origin and definition, 17–19
Brexit, xxi–xxii, 2, 5, 13, 19, 82–83, 86, 95–96, 98, 100
  motivations behind, 77–79
British Broadcasting Corporation (BBC), xx, 3, 18, 36, 86, 90, 106
  and bias, xviii, 2, 6, 8, 53
  influence, 17
Brown, Gordon, xvii, 34, 60, 77

Cameron, David, 18, 61, 83, 105
celebrity, 93–94, 98
Church of England, 3, 6, 74, 81
climate change, xix, 12–13, 17
Cobley, Ben, 10, 70, 75
Cold War, 4, 35–36, 38–39, 70
college. *See* universities
communism, 10, 30, 36–37, 45
communists, 24–25
Conservative Party, 6–7, 19, 31, 75, 100
  and the 2019 General Election, 1
  in government, xiii, 8–10
  support for, 5
ConservativeHome, 2, 61, 103
Conservatives, 6–7, 9, 95
  and the 2019 General Election, 4
Corbyn, Jeremy, 95, 100, 102
  and the 2019 General Election, 1, 3–4
  beliefs, 3, 30
  celebrity endorsements of, 93
cultural hegemony, xv–xvi, xxiii, 3, 25, 51
cultural Marxism, xv, 3–4, 10, 24, 28, 68
culture industry, 22–23, 26

culture war, xx, 4, 8–9, 14, 39, 91
Cummings, Dominic, xviii, 77–78, 81, 83, 105–106

Daily Telegraph, 2, 5, 18, 60, 72, 102
Davison Hunter, James, 91–92, 95–96, 98
Dreher, Rod, 90–91
Dutschke, Rudi, xvi, 47, 49–50

environmentalism, 19, 48, 74–75
European Union, 71–72, 78

Fabian Society, xvii, 31, 34, 52, 60, 93, 95–96, 102
  early influence, 32–33
fascism, xx, 23, 25, 30
Fischer, Joschka, 41, 45–46, 48
Frankfurt School, xvi, xx, xxii, 10, 24, 29, 39, 41, 43–44, 92
  early influence, 26–28, 96
Freudomarxism, xv–xvi, 27–28, 43
Friedman, Milton, xxi, 15, 52, 96

globalisation, 58, 100
Gove, Michael, 18, 77, 107
  and environmentalism, 12, 17
Gramsci, Antonio, xv–xvi, xx, 1–3, 10, 44–45, 47
  life, 25–26
Gramscian (political theory), xvi, 6, 45, 51, 99, 102
Gray, John, 2–3, 5, 7, 78
Gurri, Martin, 82–83, 92

Hall, Stuart, 51–52, 55
Havel, Václav, 84–87, 91–92
Hayek, Friedrich von, 52, 95, 105
higher education. *See* universities
Hitler, Adolf, xv, 23–24, 27, 47
Horkheimer, Max, xv, 22, 27–29

identity politics, 4, 68
IfS. *See* Institut für Sozialforschung (IfS)

111